I0756372

The Worst-Case Survival Book For Disaster Preparedness

THE UNCONVENTIONAL PREPPERS GUIDE TO BUG-IN FOR THE COMING SOCIETAL BREAKDOWN & POWER GRID COLLAPSE IN AS LITTLE AS 30 DAYS.

Small Footprint Press

BEFORE YOU START READING, DOWNLOAD YOUR FREE BONUSES!

Scan the QR-code & Access
all the Resources for FREE!

https://dl.bookfunnel.com/h8hzy33mn7

The Self-Sufficient Living Cheat Sheet

10 Simple Steps to Become More Self-Sufficient in 1 Hour or Less

---

How to restore balance to the environment around you... even if you live in a tiny apartment in the city.

Discover:

- **How to increase your income** by selling “useless” household items
- The environmentally friendly way to replace your car — invest in THIS special vehicle to **eliminate your carbon footprint**

- The secret ingredient to **turning your backyard into a thriving garden**

- 17+ different types of food scraps and 'waste' that you can use to feed your garden

- How to drastically **cut down on food waste** without eating less

- 4 natural products you can use to make your own eco-friendly cleaning supplies

- The simple alternative to 'consumerism' — the age-old method for **getting what you need without paying money for it**

- The 9 fundamental items you need to create a self-sufficient first-aid kit

- One of the top skills that most people are afraid of learning — and how you can master it effortlessly

- 3 essential tips for **gaining financial independence**

The Prepper Emergency Preparedness & Survival Checklist:

10 Easy Things You Can Do Right Now to Ready Your Family & Home for Any Life-Threatening Catastrophe

---

Natural disasters demolish everything in their path, but your peace of mind and sense of safety don't have to be among them. Here's what you need to know...

- Why having an emergency plan in place is so crucial and how it will help to keep your family safe

- How to stockpile emergency supplies intelligently and why you shouldn't overdo it

- How to store and conserve water so that you know you'll have enough to last you through the crisis
- A powerful 3-step guide to ensuring financial preparedness, no matter what happens
- A step-by-step guide to maximizing your storage space, so you and your family can have exactly what you need ready and available at all times
- Why knowing the hazards of your home ahead of time could save a life and how to steer clear of these in case of an emergency
- Everything you need to know for creating a successful evacuation plan, should the worst happen and you need to flee safely

101 Recipes, Tips, Crafts, DIY Projects and More for a Beautiful Low Waste Life

Reduce Your Carbon Footprint and Make Earth-Friendly Living Fun With This Comprehensive Guide

---

Practical, easy ways to improve your personal health and habits while contributing to a brighter future for yourself and the planet

Discover:

- **Simple customizable recipes for creating your own food, home garden, and skincare products**
- The tools you need for each project to successfully achieve sustainable living

- Step-by-step instructions for life-enhancing skills from preserving food to raising your own animals and forging for wild berries

- **Realistic life changes that reduce your carbon-footprint while saving you money**

- Sustainable crafts that don't require any previous knowledge or expertise

- Self-care that extends beyond the individual and positively impacts the environment

- **Essential tips on how to take back control of your life -- become self-sustained and independent**

First Aid Fundamentals

A Step-By-Step Illustrated Guide to the Top 10 Essential First Aid Procedures Everyone Should Know

---

Discover:

- **What you should do to keep this type of animal attack from turning into a fatal allergic reaction**
- Why sprains are more than just minor injuries, and how you can keep them from getting worse
- **How to make the best use of your environment in critical situations**

- The difference between second- and third-degree burns, and what you should do when either one happens

- Why treating a burn with ice can actually cause more damage to your skin

- When to use heat to treat an injury, and when you should use something cold

- **How to determine the severity of frostbite**, and what you should do in specific cases

- Why knowing this popular disco song could help you save a life

- The key first aid skill that everyone should know — **make sure you learn THIS technique the right way**

Food Preservation Starter Kit

10 Beginner-Friendly Ways to Preserve Food at Home | Including Instructional Illustrations and Simple Directions

---

Grocery store prices are skyrocketing! It's time for a self-sustaining lifestyle.

Discover:

- **10 incredibly effective and easy ways to preserve your food for a self-sustaining lifestyle**
- The art of canning and the many different ways you can preserve food efficiently without any prior experience

- A glorious trip down memory lane to learn the historical methods of preservation passed down from one generation to the next

- **How to make your own pickled goods**: enjoy the tanginess straight from your kitchen

- Detailed illustrations and directions so you won't feel lost in the preservation process

- The health benefits of dehydrating your food and how fermentation can be **the key to a self-sufficient life**

- **The secrets to living a processed-free life** and saving Mother Earth all at the same time

Download all your resources by scanning the QR-Code below:

https://dl.bookfunnel.com/h8hzy33mn7

CONTENTS

"Extinction is the rule. Survival is the exception."

- Carl Sagan

INTRODUCTION

You will, no doubt, have many reasons for becoming a prepper. In recent years, we have seen the effects of climate change in our backyards, from floods to fires to rising food prices. At the same time, we are watching as the fat cats at the top steal and pillage, leaving little for those at the bottom.

It is just a matter of time before solar flares, financial disasters, storms, hurricanes, earthquakes, and pandemics become a normal way of living for us. Unfortunately, many non-preppers may want to go on believing that things will turn out okay after all, but rising sea levels, melting glaciers, hotter temperatures, and new viruses tell a different story.

The truth of the matter is that, in this new world about to descend on us, the 'haves' and the 'have nots' will be even more clearly divided. Unlike the world we have now, in the new world, the 'haves' will be preppers: those who had the good sense to prepare for a disaster before it finally came.

We are all holding on to human civilization by a thread. You will have noticed people still buying their flat-screen TVs and heavily processed foods, ignoring the evidence right before their eyes. But you know the truth, that both you and your family are in danger.

It may not seem like it to people who are too busy entertaining their lives away, but, as an astute prepper, you know that hundreds of potentially life-threatening situations can change life as we know it–even in an instant. Those in the know realize that prepping is the only way to be truly prepared for anything: it is the only way that gives us the best chance of survival.

Let's face it, you have no excuse not to prepare for disaster. This is the easiest time in history to be a prepper, thanks to technological advances and recent developments in the prepping community, developments that we will share with you in subsequent chapters. As a prepper, you have no excuse not to take control over disaster by preparing well for yourself and your family.

To support you on your journey and give you that much-needed sense of control over your environment, we have written this detailed and essential preparation guidebook to give you back control. Not only will you gain back control over your survival with this comprehensive guide, but you will also ward off terror and fear of the unknown. You will find that once you understand how to prepare for disaster, the fear of doom will no longer control you.

In essence, this book aims to free you from fear by teaching you practical skills for survival. So, how will we achieve this? Simple. We know you are a survivor. What we want to do is help you on your way to unlocking your natural capabilities by educating you on the steps you need to take to achieve this. These are easy-to-remember steps presented through the P.O.S.S.E.S.S framework.

- ***P****racticing* self-reliance always.

- **O**btaining traditional cooking and medical skills.

- **S**toring food and water securely and safely.

- **S**ynthesizing an off-grid waste system.

- ***E***quipping yourself for self-defense against threats.

- **S**urviving when shit hits the fan.

- **S**urviving disaster and collapse.

This framework empowers you to check how many essential survival skills you have picked up for when disaster comes or shit really hits the fan! Indeed, as you go through this book, you will find that each chapter presents you with a similar framework to help you easily find the answers you are seeking. Each framework is there to bring you a memorable answer to all your prepper problems.

By reading this book, you will first learn how to start your journey of living off-grid and how to prepare for a variety of catastrophes or events which would require self-sufficiency. You will also learn other essential skills that you need to survive in a disaster. Each chapter represents a distinct element of prepping that you will need to consider to be well-prepared, as well as tips on implementing this effectively.

Not just content with bringing you tips and guides, we will also aim to give you "practices" for disasters. We will illustrate to you prepping scenarios for a variety of disasters, including information on how prepping in advance may save your life in those situations. We will also bring you practical guidance on how to ensure that you have constant water and food supplies in whatever disaster scenario you find yourself in.

Don't fret! We know you want to protect yourself and your family, so we are here to teach you how by bringing you the basics of self-defense strategies and essential weaponry. Expect to learn the pros and cons of different types of shelter, for the wilderness and for home, as well as the how-to for making a 72-hour kit bag with all the essentials that you need.

By the end of this book, you will be able to create your own emergency plan, including different roles for yourself and your family. In addition, you will be introduced to the concept of homesteading, with tips on how you can start to implement this in your own home.

Also, all the guidance and tips in this book are specifically tailored so that they can be used anywhere in the world. We aim to reach as many preppers as possible, so we have also ensured that our tips and guidance can be followed by all preppers, regardless of income level.

You will not find us recommending unnecessary high-tech or expensive survival equipment. Rather, we believe the core value of the survival prepper is to keep it as simple as possible, using as many everyday items as possible to improve your chances of survival.

We recognize that you may have done some previous research of your own on disaster prepping, so we are not here to bring you the standard disaster prepping advice. Instead, we have come prepared with new, inexpensive solutions to many of your disaster prep problems–solutions that you will find nowhere else. You can expect to gain insightful knowledge of unusual prepping techniques, many of which may be new and exciting to you.

You are not alone. Whatever your reason for prepping, you can be assured that you have picked up the perfect book that will keep you one step ahead of disaster. By the end of this book, you will feel more confident in your preparations for any disaster that may befall your part of the world and will be able to cope with a variety of situations that would catch out even experienced preppers.

Many more people are seeing the light these days and realizing the extreme benefits of being a prepper. Indeed, even celebrities, with all their wealth and connections, are coming to their senses and becoming preppers. Celebrities like Ryan Seacrest, Jamie Lee Curtis, Roseanne Barr, Zooey Deschanel, and Nathan Fillion are all self-proclaimed preppers who have all seen the need. They know that their wealth and connections will not be enough to survive. After all, disaster is the great equalizer!

When push comes to shove and we all have to survive, it is every man and woman for themselves. So, if you're ready to begin your prepping journey and to become more self-reliant, more self-assured, more confident, and less anxious, then let's begin! You are the fittest and you will survive, beginning with learning the different disaster scenarios which every prepper may face.

Who is Small Footprint Press?

Small Footprint Press, established amidst the pandemic, is a self-publishing company of experts that aims to promote sustainable survival–equipping you to live a sustainable, conscious, and independent lifestyle to make the world a better place for yourself and future generations to come.

As the world progresses, we believe that the importance of sustainable survival becomes more and more evident. Our planet faces various challenges, including climate change, dwindling resources, population growth, and pandemics. To secure a bright future for our children *now* is the time we must take steps to save our planet.

We accomplish this by simply empowering you to prepare for potential disasters for yourself and your loved ones. Gone are the days when you stress about the day of the unknown!

Our books are a collaboration of different authors, each with their perspective and expertise. This makes for a well-rounded book that covers various topics in depth, ensuring the highest quality standards. It also makes for a more engaging read, as each author brings their unique style to the table.

Similarly, orchestras comprise different instruments, each with its unique sound and purpose. Once these instruments play as one in harmony, the result is extraordinary.

We believe that one way to bridge a community of people with a shared purpose and values is through books! In this community, you will build genuine relationships, share similar experiences, and be empowered to take action.

You are not alone. There's something special about a journey taken with others. Whether exploring a new city or embarking on a long hike, sharing the experience with others makes you enjoy the journey more than the destination.

So allow us to join you in your journey to a compelling life of sustainable survival! Interested in joining our cause? Download your FREE resources at the beginning of the book!

CHAPTER ONE: PREPPING 101

If you are new to disaster preparation, you may ask yourself what it is all about. Sure, you have a general idea of what it entails, but what exactly does being a "prepper" mean? Does it mean preparing for the end of the world, pandemics, war, or natural disasters?

There are so many forms of disaster that, for a beginner, it may be difficult to pinpoint what exactly this community is about. Believe it or not, some people even prep for a zombie apocalypse! So how do we narrow down what we mean when we say "prepper"? Well, using the framework P.R.E.P.P.E.R, you can easily understand that prepping empowers you to:

- ***P***rotect yourself and your loved ones.
- ***R***isk-assess your chance of survival when disaster strikes.
- ***E***vade deep pain and suffering caused by a disaster.

- ***P***osition yourself as a leader in the community.

- ***P***repare yourself mentally for survival.

- ***E***ncourage your natural human instinct for survival.

- ***R***espond to threats with appropriate force.

As you read through this chapter, you will find ways in which being a P.R.E.P.P.E.R helps you find common life-saving solutions against disaster and its accompanying problems. The one thing you can tell from the framework is that a prepper does not hide from the harsh truths and cold realities of the world. A prepper knows that civilizations, societies, and communities can, and have, collapsed in the past—whether temporarily or permanently.

Rather than leave it up to chance and false hope that they will never face a collapse in their lifetime, a prepper stands tall to take control of their life. A prepper values their survival, and hence, does the hard work necessary to survive. A prepper knows that the civilizations we humans build for ourselves are precarious at best. One flood, one night of riots, or one pandemic is all it takes to wipe it all away for an extended period.

Being a prepper is simply common sense. You are honoring and following your natural human instinct for survival, an instinct that has been developed and fine-tuned over many generations.

So, whether you prepare for water scarcity, food scarcity, financial difficulties, self-defense, a pandemic, security, loss of power, or even a zombie apocalypse, what matters is that you are following your natural human instinct for survival because you never know when the system will fail you and you will need a back-up plan.

We can say, then, that a prepper is a responsible, enterprising risk-assessor who creates their own survival insurance against a rainy day. One of the easiest ways to become a prepper is to follow a preparedness pyramid. A preparedness pyramid is a pyramid that shows you all the different emergencies you can prepare for. It works like any other pyramid.

On the bottom are the most basic/common events to prepare for based on the likelihood of them happening. Nearing the top are those events that are less likely to occur but will need more extensive preparation if you are to survive.

A preparedness pyramid is typically structured into these five levels, with level 1 at the base and level 5 at the peak:

1. Basic prepping

Basic prepping is prepping for basic emergencies that will be typically resolved after a few hours or days at most. For example, having emergency flashlights at home in case of a sudden power outage. Basic prepping is also for everyday emergencies that you are so used to that you may not even consider them being emergencies, such as ensuring you have some cash on you at all times in case you cannot use your debit/credit card.

2. Temporary setbacks

Temporary setbacks typically set us back a few weeks or months before we can bounce back. Your roof may need extensive repairs, or you may need to be off work for a couple of weeks. Temporary setbacks typically have a low financial impact and can be solved with an emergency fund.

3. Weather, recession and injuries

Weather, recession, and injuries can be classified as more serious setbacks. They can set you back months and even years. A freak storm could cause you to lose your home, for example, or you may need to be admitted into hospital for a few months, unable to work. The best prep method for these disasters is, of course, insurance.

4. Disaster and collapse

What happens if society collapses? What happens if you experience a major financial/geopolitical crisis or a natural disaster? Your primary worry would be how you would survive the first night and subsequent nights after.

Imagine you hear that enemy troops are marching into your city. You need to head for the nearest border. You will save plenty of time if you already have your survival kit packed for the future, including supplies to last you during the treacherous journey.

When preparing for disaster and collapse, you need to ensure you can survive a week without regular amenities, such as working supermarkets selling food and readily available running water. Let us give you a scenario: if the national grid is damaged thanks to a flood, then you will still have electricity until the issue is fixed thanks to your prior preparation!

Let's look at another scenario: perhaps you need to evacuate to a safer area after an earthquake but are trapped thanks to rubble. You have enough supplies to last a couple of weeks. However, you will need other things apart from food and drink if you are to meet your needs. If you are trapped in a disaster zone, one of the greatest tools for survival that you will have at your disposal is information. But what happens if you have no means of communicating with the outside world because the electricity is down? In this case, a power bank will help you charge your phone and any other devices that you can use to communicate with the outside world. Indeed, your power bank could end up saving your life if you have enough power in your mobile phone to reach emergency/rescue services.

As the disastrous effects of climate change become a regular occurrence and geopolitical tensions rise all over the world, a level four preparation is a matter of life and death.

Conversely, while disaster preparation requires short-term planning, surviving a financial or political collapse requires long-term planning. After society collapses, you can no longer rely on the government and on businesses to provide you with stability. By preparing, you offer yourself stability in an unstable world.

For example, an emergency fund (a stash of physical cash) could help you to purchase food during an economic depression, especially if bank cards stop working. The fact is that collapse brings with it less reliable power, an unstable supply of drinking water, and very little food. Hence, the more self-sufficient you are, the more likely you are to survive. In the case of collapse, self-sufficiency includes things like growing your own food, having an emergency food stash, and having a way to filter water and make it safe for drinking (as discussed further in other chapters).

5. SHTF (Shit Hits The Fan)

Level five, or "shit hits the fan" helps you prepare for the worst that could possibly happen. This could be things like a deadly pandemic, a nuclear disaster, or a deep societal collapse where civilization has completely broken down. This is usually the case when war breaks out or international conflict escalates, resulting in war crimes, something we have seen happen more and more in recent decades. In this scenario, there is no law, and it is truly survival of the fittest.

Have you seen those disaster movies where one man or woman is trying to survive in a post-collapse or post-apocalyptic world? You will notice that the protagonist is always well-prepared while characters who aren't well-prepared usually die at the beginning of the movie. The same happens in real life. Those who survived war zones in Europe during the 20th century often had one of two things on their side: (1) being prepared and (2) luck.

Another important reason for being well-prepared is that when the shit hits the fan, go back to the most primitive survival methods humans have. Unfortunately, we rely on technology too much nowadays. The problem with our reliance on technology is that technology requires a lot of processes to keep it working.

Even the simplest part not working can cause everything to shut down. So, a wealthy oligarch might think they are fine in their fortress, complete with a cinema, two double-door fridges, and the highest speed internet. But if the electric generator stops working, and they don't know how to fix it or are not prepared with the tools needed to fix it, the shit really will hit the fan.

A good prepper prepares for all eventualities and is certain of survival, even when technology fails. During a disaster, the everyday tools we take for granted become as precious as gold. You may have a gun for shooting prey for food, however, you won't want to waste a finite number of bullets on killing a rabbit for dinner. As a result, a simple rope and knife will become your most prized possessions since they help you trap and kill animals for food.

As a prepper, it is important to begin with the base of the pyramid because preparing for the basics gives you a chance of surviving any doomsday scenario. For example, packing basic survival gear like batteries, water, and a first aid kit will keep you alive longer than not doing so, no matter the situation you are in.

Levels 1-3 are regarded as "common sense" preparation among preppers. It is common sense to have insurance in case of emergencies. It is also common sense to have emergency funds to cover temporary setbacks in life. This book will focus on level 4 (disaster/collapse) and level 5 (SHTF) because these emergencies require more than "common sense." They require more expert skills and knowledge reserved only for those intelligent enough to seek it.

WHAT AM I PREPPING FOR?

Reading the beginning of this chapter, you can already tell that there are different disaster scenarios that you may face at any moment. Likewise, you know by now that there are wonderful benefits of prepping for survival and becoming self-reliant. But before you can determine what to prep, you must first understand what you are prepping for. To determine the cure, you must first diagnose the illness to know what challenges you are facing. So, what are you prepping for?

There are six major disasters that preppers typically prepare for. They are:

1. **Natural disasters**

The first thing that comes to mind when prepping for disaster is probably natural disasters. Natural disasters are a big part of the human experience, occurring with alarming frequency. As climate change worsens, we have seen bigger and more frequent natural disasters. From floods, to earthquakes, to hurricanes, to forest fires, natural disasters can destroy entire countries. They can also disrupt your power supply, communication, and food and water supply for a long time. Undeniably, they are a serious issue.

2. Artificial disasters

Artificial disasters are a much sadder experience than natural disasters because they are most often needlessly and accidentally caused. It is always best to treat artificial disasters as seriously as natural disasters because of their ability to destroy almost everything immediately.

Sometimes, artificial disasters can be more dangerous than natural disasters. One of the most destructive disasters that can befall any prepper is a nuclear power meltdown or a bomb explosion. These disasters are so dangerous, particularly because they have the power to cause deep pain and suffering, even for generations.

Think about how people say that it is better to die in a nuclear explosion than to live with the effects of radiation poisoning. The problem is, you don't get a say in that and you could have to face the consequences of surviving the initial blast.

Conversely, there are so many ways for a bomb explosion to hurt you, for example, glass shards exploding and hurling themselves into your body at full speed. There is hope, however, if you know how to protect yourself from the effects of artificial disasters, then you reduce your chances and intensity of pain and suffering.

What we can say definitely is that artificial disasters are just as dangerous as natural ones and should be taken just as seriously.

3. Social unrest

Social unrest is a constant threat to your survival. It usually manifests as protests, riots, walkouts, or wars. During times of social unrest, you cannot rely on society to work like clockwork, so your normal way of life becomes threatened. Take, for example, a nationwide truckers' strike. Truckers decide to walk out on a national scale for better conditions. As a result, food distribution becomes affected, leading to empty aisles at the supermarket.

If you are prepped with food to last you until the strike is over, you won't have to panic buy or become anxious when you cannot find any food at the supermarket. Let's take another example. If you and your family suddenly find yourselves near a bomb explosion and chaos erupts, you could easily become separated. There is safety in numbers, and separation also increases your chances of further disaster happening to one or more of you.

However, if you plan on what to do during emergencies, your training will kick in even during the chaos, and you can all stay safe together.

4. Biological warfare

Most countries today have nukes and biochemical weapons. We have seen, in recent years, that some national leaders are not scared of using these weapons against their own people and they wouldn't hesitate to use them as threats. If you want to survive, you must consider modern health hazards and prepare adequately for them.

5. Financial challenges

Saving has become a lost art today. Everyone wants to buy, buy, buy, but forget that there will come a time when they face financial difficulties. As a prepper, you are smart enough to resist the status quo, so you work hard to be free of debt in every way. You pour your money into canned food, gardening, green housing, and other ways to keep you alive when you meet future financial challenges. You are also savvy enough to recognize that it is much cheaper and much more self-reliant to produce your own food.

Sometimes, financial challenges come because of wider societal or financial problems that are not your fault. Rightfully, in these cases, you cannot control the value of your currency/currencies. However, a prepper knows that you must also stock up with things that can be used as barter if money becomes valueless.

6. Personal challenges

Life is filled with ups and downs. We all wish it was filled with just ups–in which case you wouldn't need to prep. A wise person sees the warning signs of trouble in the future and prepares for it. A foolish person blindly looks away and pretends it will not affect them. In fact, a foolish person will tell you that preparing for disaster is simply an overreaction.

However, even if you are lucky enough to avoid a major level 4 or 5 disaster, prepping is still a great idea because it allows you to survive the personal challenges with less stress and pain. Either way, the wise person wins!

Prepping for personal challenges is even more imperative if you have young children or other vulnerable people who depend on you. We hate to say it, but the truth is that we live in a 'dog eat dog world.' Nobody will come to rescue you or your family if you suffer personal challenges that set you back.

The fat cats in power often like to act as though they care just to get our votes. They often manipulate us into buying their products and creating more wealth for them by working in their factories. They make promises, but always disappoint us at the worst possible moment. Those in power will never come to your aid. Indeed, what will more than likely happen is that you will be blamed despite being a victim yourself.

As a prepper, you are too self-reliant to have your hand out to the government because you know they will fail you.

On the other hand, ordinary people will never turn against more powerful men and women. So, when you prep and shoulder personal challenges, you do not need to rely on anyone for help to get back up or survive. You show others you belong to a class of powerful people. Your strength immediately and naturally demands other people's respect, and as a result, your confidence soars.

Every single person on this Earth will face at least one of these events in their lifetime. It is safe to say we will probably all face more than one of these events in our lifetime. Since we live in a world where only the fittest survive, you are technically descended from the fittest. It is in your genes to survive!

In essence, we are the children of strong survivors and warriors. Therefore, it is nothing but an insult to take modern conveniences and technology for granted and waste your time sitting on the couch, eating a delivered pizza, and wasting electricity watching shows with no value on TV.

To honor those ancestors who suffered so you could be here today, it is your human duty to work hard to continue to use the survival skills that are now embedded in your DNA and to learn new skills that will enable your great-great-great-grandchild to survive too.

One of the greatest examples of not honoring your survival instinct happened during the COVID-19 pandemic. We all saw the footage of people fighting, scrambling, and rushing just to buy a 6-pack of toilet paper, a bottle of water, alcohol, and sanitizers. Before that, preppers were seen by the world as conspiracy nuts. But those of us who knew were not worried about that because we had a sense of dignity and personal pride.

Once people faced the almost apocalyptic nightmare of trying to survive during COVID, respect for our intelligence and our dignity grew. Here is what one journalist wrote during the height of the pandemic:

"You've heard of preppers, right? Survivalists? You know about their strange, apocalyptic beliefs: that a disaster could strike at any time, overwhelming first responders and the social safety net; that this crisis could disrupt supply chains, causing scarcity and panic and social breakdown; that authorities might invoke emergency powers and impose police curfews. Crazy theories like that.

"In fact, many perfectly reputable organizations—including the US federal government and the Red Cross—rccommend Americans maintain extra food and emergency supplies. The Federal Emergency Management Agency (FEMA) advises keeping a two-week supply of food, as well as water, batteries, medical masks, first-aid supplies, and a battery-or hand-powered radio, among other things.

"In mainstream society, however, interest in prepping usually invites ridicule about bunkers and tin-foil hats. Preppers have spent years as the objects of our collective derision.

"Until now. Today, we're all preppers—or rather, wish we had been. Non-preppers have been caught in a rain shower without an umbrella. I don't know if preppers are laughing right now, but perhaps they're entitled to some vindication.

But I've come to respect the preppers' ethos of survival and preparedness. One of my friends is one, or at least on the spectrum. When coronavirus hit, he wasn't one of the millions of people scrambling for surgical masks; he already had them in his survival kit. He kept a few and gave the rest to elderly people" (Conroy, 2020).

If, by some chance, you still aren't convinced, here are some other compelling reasons for becoming a prepper:

1. You strengthen your community

Despite the COVID-19 pandemic, many people still aren't preppers today. After the buying and hoarding madness during the early months of the pandemic, most people were so desperate to return to normal that they forgot all about the usefulness of prepping, especially in case of another (inevitable) disaster.

As you saw in the article above, the prepper in that situation was able to take care of his community by providing surgical masks to the vulnerable in the community. When you are a prepper, you are a leader of your community because you are a chance for survival and a beacon of hope for those around you.

This may seem like an exaggeration, but think about it. If you have your own farm and can feed your neighbors' children during civil unrest, you become a beacon of hope for your neighbors until the unrest ends and they can go out and buy some more food. This leads us to the second reason why preppers are so useful to the world.

2. You foster peace and wellbeing

Think of the panic in your community if people cannot feed their children, the elderly, babies, pets, and any other vulnerable people? Think of how people may get desperate and resort to crime and violence. However, if you can provide rations, supplies, and tools, peace is restored in your community temporarily until authorities can restore a more stable peace and stability.

During the Blitz in London, Londoners often huddled in the underground to avoid German bomber planes. One particular time, a nursing mother was stuck with other mothers and children for weeks. Food was scarce and there would not be enough for even the children. The mothers decided to feed the nursing mother alone instead so that she could breastfeed all the babies and the children.

Because of their quick thinking and putting their supplies to good use, the crisis was averted. While it may not be wise (or legal) for every prepper in the world to keep a nursing mother in case of emergencies, raising animals is a great alternative for providing constant food, sustenance, and nutrition in times of crisis.

You also foster peace when you store goods—by not needing to panic buy in times of disaster. The more preppers in a society, the fewer people will be out and about panic buying. In turn, there will be more supplies to go around, thereby reducing the air of panic and fear among those who have not prepped and are desperate for supplies.

Benefits Of Prepping

We have already inadvertently covered some of the benefits of prepping in this chapter, namely because they are so numerous. Likewise, here are some more surprising benefits of being a prepper:

1. **Boosts your confidence**

Being a prepper gives you a confidence boost and affects all other areas of your life. When you are a prepper, you essentially train yourself to be a leader; you teach yourself how to be responsible, even in moments of chaos. In the process, you also train yourself to be calm and to focus on what you and others need to do to survive.

This stoicism and responsibility naturally draw others to you, making you a leader. As a naturally elected leader, your self-confidence will rise and begin to affect other areas of your life, such as your work, your relationships, and your finances. Since people trust you for something as important as their survival, it makes you feel more capable and more trustworthy. Soon, you begin to act accordingly.

Confidence breeds success, which, in turn, reinforces your confidence. In any case, it is a win-win situation.

2. Your relationship with your family deepens

Thanks to your newfound confidence, your relationship with your family gets better. Doing drills together and prepping together also helps you spend time and bond. Finally, your family will feel happy and supported to know that you care enough about them to include them in your disaster preparation plans.

a. You feel less stressed and anxious on a day-to-day basis knowing that you and your family are prepared and protected.

b. You enjoy yourself.

The more you prep, the more you try new things that you may not have tried otherwise. You may want to try gardening or having your own greenhouse, to wean yourself from your reliance on supermarkets. You may also try animal husbandry (raising animals), fishing, camping, and hunting—earning you a new hobby sooner or later.

Prepping is a great way to stimulate your mind, stop boredom and even meet new people. There is always something else you can learn to improve your preparedness and survival skills, some of which will require you to meet with other people, such as learning how to fire a gun or learning how to hunt.

Even better, the more you socialize with strangers, the more likely your bartering and negotiation skills will also improve—skills you will need to survive a disaster. Think about how convincing someone to trust you enough to give you a lift during mass civil unrest could be the deciding factor in whether you survive or die.

3. You get fitter

You will need to be fit to survive in case of a disaster. You can't run from advancing enemy troops, for example, if you have not kept yourself in great shape before disaster strikes. Hence, prepping keeps you healthy, especially if you switch to growing and/or rearing your own organic produce.

a. You get the satisfaction of one day being the hero who saves others with your exceptional leadership skills.

b. Financial rewards.

You can make money on the side by selling produce from your gardens or your farm animals. You can also sell any surplus supplies you don't need (once you take care of your family and the vulnerable in your community).

Growing your own produce saves you money as does learning to fix things on your own. You will also need to learn to stay fit through natural means, instead of relying on the modern convenience of a gym, as you will need to continue to keep fit even during a disaster so that you can run or fight for your life at any moment's notice. As a result, you can save on a gym membership too.

4. **You develop your survival instincts**

Performing regular disaster preparedness drills will help you hone your fight-or-flight skills, which come in handy for protecting you in everyday life, for example, helping you avoid accidents or avoid dangerous people.

5. **You learn to appreciate nature**

Being a prepper means learning to be at one with nature. Our great-grandparents and their great-grandparents survived thanks to nature. Nature has herbs for healing; the wood for fire and warmth and for making survival tools; the berries, fruits, vegetables and mushrooms for energy; the trees for shade, for constructing shelter and hiding from enemies; the rivers for cleaning and bathing; the wildlife for hunting and so on.

It has also been scientifically proven that spending time in nature is great for our mental and emotional health (O'Hare, 2019). The more time you spend in nature learning and honing your survival skills, and building your bug-out location, the more happy and content you will become. This will also benefit other areas of your life, like your work and your relationships.

5 Things To Avoid As A Prepper

1. **Relying on your gear instead of your skills**

While your gear is important, having the skills to use it correctly during a disaster is even more important. Without your skills, your gear is useless: you may have a gun, but if you don't know how to use it, you won't be able to protect yourself. Likewise, with knowledge of your skills, you still have a good chance of survival because you will know how to build makeshift tools instead. To survive, you will need the following skills:

- Preparing food
- Preparing water
- Combat
- Using weapons and firearms

- Building, preparing, and caretaking an off-grid home.
- First aid and basic medical skills
- Growing food and raising livestock
- Hunting

There are many skills that you will need as a prepper. The best way to gain them all is to go through different scenarios that you may encounter as a prepper and jot down all the skills you will need to survive that scenario.

2. Not being prepared

Imagine this scenario: A disaster has happened and gangs have started looting people's homes. You have a reputation for being a prepper, which means you are in danger. You hear someone coming down your street, so you rush upstairs to get your defensive gear only to find that it is still in its packaging and you do not know how to use it. Make sure you are prepared and know how to use your equipment properly.

It would be ironic to be a prepper and not be prepared on the day of an emergency.

Another tip for being prepared is to read as many books on prepping as you can. What's more, keep the most important ones for use during times of a disaster. For example, you may need to fix a very specific problem with your off-grid waste management system. The information for fixing it may be too niche for you to remember, so having the book on hand during a crisis could become a lifesaver!

3. Inadequate food or water

Be careful not to underestimate how much water and food you will need in survival mode. Humans can typically survive much longer without food. However, you have a maximum of three days without water before you die. So you must be extra careful when prepping to ensure that you are prepped for water supply. As a general rule of thumb, an average person needs two gallons of water per day.

As with all preparation for survival, you want to prep so that you have enough rationed for two weeks. This means that you will need to store a lot of water. Especially if you are on the run, you will need to have a way to purify water.

It's generally best to have a few days of water with you and then the means to purify water as well. That way you have some water to drink while you try to find a source of water if you already do not have one.

Another way to prep for water is to map out areas within your vicinity that have good sources of water, such as rivers and lakes, and use a purification kit. You can then get water from these sources purified and have enough water for survival.

Last, you may want to invest in water-catching devices that can store water from the rain.

When storing food, don't get carried away with only storing the staples like beans and flour. While these are great for energy, you also need a wide source and variety of food to get all your minerals and vitamins in. Store multivitamins to help you power your brain, ward off fatigue, anxiety, and sickness, and cope with stress.

Your body just cannot eat the same food over and over again. Eventually, it will shut down and reject eating the same food. This is why it's important to learn how to grow your own food and even keep livestock, because you're then able to have a wide variety of nutrients from food.

You can stock up on minerals and vitamins because you can then take these once in a while if your body is not willing to eat the food that you have stored or you don't have a food source that contains certain essential vitamins or minerals.

You may also want to map out the surrounding area to note the best sources of berries, edible mushrooms, fish, medicinal plants, and animals. Don't forget to stock up on seasoning herbs, salt, and more because eating food without seasoning is a miserable existence!

If you store large amounts of water, make sure that you're using it within at least three days to avoid contamination and disease. Follow a similar rule for food. Keep a detailed account of when you store food so that you can always eat food with the closest expiration date. This way, you prevent wasting food during a time of disaster when even the smallest bit of food could be the difference between life and death. Likewise, you do not want to eat expired food unknowingly, as you want to avoid being even mildly sick during a disaster/apocalypse.

4. **Under-preparing or over-preparing**

As a prepper, you can easily fall into the trap of over-preparing for food and water, ignoring other important things that you must prepare for as a result. If you have type 1 diabetes, for example, you need to ensure that you have enough insulin to survive for a few months. You also want to ensure that you prepare for medical emergencies in the form of a first aid kit. Likewise, you want to have adequate ways to start a fire, like matches.

Do you have a torch for an emergency light supply? Do you have an emergency sleeping bag, cooking equipment, blankets, and clothing? Do you have sunscreen and sun-protective clothing? These are all important things you need to take into consideration when prepping to ensure that you are not under-prepared. Even the smallest under-preparation or over-preparation could be the defining factor between life and death; between being saved and being left behind.

You don't want to fall into the trap of over-preparing for self-defense and self-protection. Yes, you need guns and ammo, but you also don't need too many bullets and guns taking up space for the essentials, like medication, food, and water. You also want to be prepared with things that you can barter with in the event of collapse when money becomes valueless. Food, water, and medication are the most valuable currency during a disaster.

Furthermore, even though you will need guns and bullets for hunting, you don't want to have it in your mind that you will easily kill people. You also need to protect your mental health. In fact, you especially need to protect your mental health because this is what will see you through a disaster or collapse. It's no small thing to kill someone, and everyone will be acting out of instinct in a disaster situation. Understand their motive and choose any form of a deterrent rather than fatally injuring someone. If, for example, someone tries to rob you of your food, rather than shooting them, bear spray or a baton will do enough damage.

Practice using different types of knives for hunting, butchering, wood chopping, and self-defense.

Lastly, don't be under-prepared for your pets. If they are city/indoor pets, they will need your help to survive during a disaster. They may not be able to walk long distances, for example, or catch their own food for survival. You must pack for their survival too, including medication, water, first aid, and clothing.

For the sake of your mental health, you must also prepare yourself for the harsh realities of owning a pet when shit hits the fan. Other survivors may target your pet as a good source. If things get really bad, you will have to eat your pet for survival.

5. Being inflexible

Unfortunately, when disaster strikes or when shit hits the fan, we cannot predict how it will unfold. There are so many variables and so many ways for a disaster to occur. That is why you just cannot have an inflexible plan. You might say that you'll meet up with your family at a certain place, but find that your car is no longer working or public transportation has stopped being operational, effective immediately.

This is why being flexible with your plans will give you a better chance of survival. This does not mean that you entirely dismiss having a special place to meet up with your family. Rather, you might have a backup plan where each family member carries an emergency phone with them at all times, so that if shit hits the fan, you're able to communicate with each other to decide on a new place to meet.

With so many ways that disaster can occur, creating as many plans as possible for disaster is a great way to be prepared.

Check-In Exercise

Before we proceed with the rest of the book, let's first explore where you are right now in your Off-Grid Journey. This exercise will help you measure how ready you would be to face disaster if it occurred right now. They are designed after each chapter in the book so that you can check in real-time how much your knowledge is increasing as you go through the chapters and what level/skill of prepping you have gained after each chapter.

Below, rate yourself on a scale of 1-5 on how accurate the statements are for you. A score of 1 means "not accurate," and a score of 5 means "very accurate." After you have rated yourself according to the statements, add the total of your scores, then read "What Your Score Really Means" to determine the outcome of your results.

Check-in Statement	**Self Rating**
I am completely sure that I can live off the grid.	
I have a detailed idea of what it takes to be self-sufficient.	

My bug-out bag contains everything I need to survive for 3 days.	
I know where I will source water and how to purify it.	
I have stored food for emergencies and am now food self-sufficient.	
I have decided whether it is best for me to bug-in or bug-out. I know how to fortify my home for bugging in and how to create my own bunker or shelter for bugging out.	
I have a basic knowledge of first aid to treat either myself or my family.	

I know how to create a basic off-grid waste system.	
I know how to keep myself safe from enemies during a disaster.	
I have an emergency plan for any disaster scenario that could happen right now.	
TOTAL SCORE:	

What Your Score Really Means

Score: 10-15

You are not prepared for a disaster and will struggle to keep yourself and your family safe during an emergency.

Don't worry! That's why this book is here. We will go through all the key points that will have you moving from a beginner to an expert.

Score: 16 - 30

You have a basic understanding of what it means to be a prepper, but you should review your strategies and make changes to enhance your preparedness.

Great job! You know the basics, and that is definitely a good start. However, you may need to make some changes to give yourself the best chance of surviving any situation.

Score: 31+

You are almost ready for survival during a disaster! Review your plans to ensure they are ready to go.

Key Chapter Takeaway

You are now on your way to becoming a prepper! You deserve heavy congratulations! To help you out, here are some key takeaways as you think about getting started on your prepping journey.

- A prepper stands tall to take control of their life when society collapses and disaster occurs.
- Being a prepper is simply common sense. You are honoring and following your natural human instinct for survival.
- The preparedness pyramid guides you on which disasters to prep for first and those to prep for last because of their likelihood of happening.

As you go through the next chapters, we would advise that you return to the check-in statements and quiz yourself periodically. Those check-in statements are designed specifically to test your ability to survive in the case of a disaster. We cannot stress enough how disaster often arrives in an instant.

We would love to live in a world where the Earth warns us of a deadly earthquake before it happens, but, alas, we don't! Even when scientists or government officials can give us warnings beforehand, you risk not being able to find an essential supply or not having enough time to learn how to use a weapon for self-defense.

Prepping is a matter of life and death. It is as simple as that. Life is divided into two unique categories: those who die and those who survive. There is no in-between. So, it is better to be safe than sorry. And what better way to do so than by judging your prepping skills at the end of every chapter, and referring to the check-in statements above to see how ready you are to face and survive a disaster if it hits you right now?

In the next chapter, you will learn how to create a bug-out bag (if you don't already have one) as the first step in your emergency response if you need to immediately leave home.

Chapter Two: Bugging Out

What is a bug-out bag? How do you prepare a bug-out bag? Whether you're new to prepping or you're more experienced, you may be wondering how to prepare a bug-out bag and what to put in a bug-out bag.

Even if you already have one, it's always a good idea to refresh your bug-out bag periodically, to ensure that it contains the things that you need to survive, depending on your location, your climate, the people in your survival party, and other outside variables. Quite simply, your bug-out bag is the first step in creating an emergency response to any scenario. This chapter will teach you how to (or, for more seasoned preppers, refresh your memory on how to):

- Identify what a bug-out bag is.
- Learn the benefits of a bug-out bag and why it's useful.

- Make a checklist of what you need in a bug-out bag.

So, we return to the fundamental question: "What is a bug-out bag?" A bug-out bag is essentially a bag made for survival. In this bag, you have all the essential things that you need to survive in a life-or-death scenario. It is meant to be big enough to contain your survival rations and equipment, but also small and light enough to be easy to carry, even in harsh weather and conditions.

So, a bug-out bag will not have your favorite bar of chocolate. It will, however, have things like a flashlight, emergency medication, such as inhalers if you are asthmatic, and water, or the means of purifying dirty water. A bug-out bag is always ready for use in case of an emergency. This means that it is always complete with everything you need and placed in an easy-to-reach position so that you can pick it up and go at any moment. A great way to remember the essential purpose of a bug-out bag is to use the BUG framework:

- ***B***e prepared to leave at any minute.
- ***U****tilize* the "survival rule of 3."
- ***G***et only what's necessary for a life-or-death scenario.

Bug-out bags typically have different names, such as the 72-hour-bag. However, their basic function is always the same.

At this point, you may be eager to know what to include in your bug-out bag. But, before we dive into this information, it is important to understand why bug-out bags are so important to have in your home and are ready to go. Why do preppers rely on bug-out bags so much?

Bug-out bags are very versatile. That means that you can prepare for any emergency. If the area in which you live is prone to severe flooding, you can prepare for floods by placing all your important documents in waterproof containers. The trick is to pack essentials that would help *you* survive.

You may not need to pack your prescription reading glasses since you don't use them, while your wife may need to pack her regular glasses since she relies on them for sight. If you live in an area where there are no natural disasters, your bug-out bag will not prepare for that. It might prepare for when *shit hits the fan,* for example, a sudden military coup.

Unfortunately, when disaster hits, time is of the essence. Every single second counts. If the government is evacuating people and you get to the evacuation point even one second too late, that could be the difference between surviving or dying. While the world may want to believe in *Kumbaya* and "positive vibes," the truth is that humans prioritize themselves over each other when in a disaster.

Our brains are designed to keep us alive at all costs—even if that means others perish. Don't be lulled into a false sense of security in case of a disaster or when shit hits the fan. The surrounding people can very easily turn against you since disaster brings about survival-of-the-fittest conditions.

So, how do you become the fittest? Well, one way is to be the fastest. In the wild, the fastest gazelle avoids the lion and can avert disaster. You must do the same. As soon as a disaster hits, you need to prioritize your time. You can't afford to spend two hours packing for everything that you need. You also can't spend an additional 30 minutes looking for one thing or another and not knowing where it is.

Imagine, for example, you are caught up in a fire. In this instance, the one thing that you need is water. If you need to walk or drive away from the fire, you will quickly become fatigued with no water. A good bug-out bag contains water to keep you alive. Remember, the B in B.U.G stands for, "**b**e prepared to leave at any minute."

Don't forget that sometimes disasters can force us to stay home. We saw this happen at the beginning of the coronavirus epidemic when we were all forced to stay indoors for long periods. Well, if you're in a lockdown, or otherwise forced to stay indoors for a long time to survive, you will need rations and survival equipment to stay alive.

You may need self-protection as well. Therefore, bug-out bags are not just for venturing out into the wild. They are also for surviving at home. We like to think about our bug-out bags as a way to take our homes with us wherever we are. If you think about it, your home contains things you need to survive on a day-to-day basis, from water to food to tools and even self-protective gear.

The bug-out bag is just a way of making your home mobile. Consequently, you find that you can use many things that you already have at home when you're trying to create your bug-out bag.

Last, bug-out bags are actually an excellent way to practice minimalism. Go into any of your neighbors' houses and you will find it filled with junk they don't need. Preppers are, by nature, anti-consumption because we know that food, water and medicine are so much more important than a new pair of designer sneakers. Without fail, we prioritize our survival, preferring to focus on what is essential in life—not what is popular.

The more you prep your bug-out bag and help others prep theirs, the more skilled you become at learning how to determine if an item is essential or not—both in everyday life and during times of disaster.

What Needs To Go In It?

Your bug-out bag must be created based on the survival rule of 3. The survival rule of 3 states that there are 3 things that you cannot survive without. They are: food, water, and air. As a result, the first things you pack into your bug-out bag should meet these needs.

Food

You can survive **3 weeks** without food.

3 weeks of food is too much to carry. In addition, your bug-out bag is purposed to help you survive the first 72 hours of a disaster, so pack enough food for 3 days. Those three days' worth of food will give you enough energy to seek out alternative sources of fresh food, whether it be through foraging, hunting, or fishing. Therefore, ensure that you pack

calorie-dense, protein-dense, and carb-dense food that can keep you energized for a long time.

You should also pack foods that contain essential micro-nutrients, such as vitamins and minerals. Without the macronutrients found in fruit and vegetables, your body will begin to deteriorate fast.

Water

You can survive **3 days** without water before you die.

Unfortunately, water is very heavy. Even carrying a 3-liter bottle will get heavy very soon. Adding a water purification system will help you purify the water on the go. You can purify water from off-grid sources like rainwater, streams, and lakes, as well as from on-grid sources, like tap water. You should also carry a water bottle or bladder that can be easily collapsed when empty, for easy, space-saving storage. Whenever you find water, you can fill up your bottle/bladder.

Air

You can survive **3 minutes** without oxygen.

You will need a handy way to purify your air in case the air becomes badly polluted, so an air filtration mask is paramount to our survival.

Other essentials you need in your bug-out bag (not based on the survival rule of 3) are:

Shelter

You can survive only **3 hours** in a harsh environment without shelter. Harsh environments include things like freezing climates, hot weather, floods, storms and more.

You will need to pack a sleeping bag, tent, space blanket, and any other items needed to create a temporary shelter.

Clothing

Perhaps clothing is just an offshoot of shelter, i.e. a way to protect your skin and body from damaging elements. Don't pack just the basics.

A shirt, trousers and a jacket might seem to be common sense, but you will also use your hands a lot in a survival situation.

Remember that humans evolved to use our hands as tools and weapons. We survived because we have dexterous fingers to accomplish complicated tasks. Hence, you want to protect your hands because they are your greatest tool for survival during a disaster. Use gloves while working, for example, while chopping wood or gathering firewood. Likewise, use gloves to protect your hands in case it gets really cold. You do not want to get frostbite on your fingers, as this will lead to serious health complications.

Likewise, protect your head from the cold with headgear-like caps and keep a change of clothes to prevent discomfort and even hypothermia from wearing damp clothes.

Heat/Warmth

The easiest way to provide heat and warmth is to start a fire. While you can easily find wood or other materials to start a fire. The problem is finding a spark. So, carry matches and other types of fire starters that can be stored safely in your bug-out bag.

If you have space, put hand warmers and foot warmers in your bug-out bag. They would be very useful in keeping you warm in freezing climates. Of course, in tropical climates, pack clothes that would enable you to regulate your body temperature. You may want to pack UV protective clothing to keep you protected from the harmful effects of UV radiation.

Power Source

You will want to keep in touch with family members, friends, and emergency services while on the move. You will also want to keep in contact with those around you to improve your chances of survival. Phone batteries run out and solar chargers won't be as effective if there is no sunlight. A fully charged, high Mah Power-Bank will provide an emergency source of electricity for charging all your other bug-out devices.

Lighting

You need light to function at night. Electricity is more than likely guaranteed to fail in a disaster, even if only temporarily. You will need light at night to carry out basic functions like cooking and using the toilet. You will also need it to protect yourself from predators and from other humans who may want to harm you.

A source of light will also enable rescue searchers to find you much easier. Chemlights, headlights, and flashlights are significant sources of light. We recommend you purchase a solar charger for your lighting sources so you can charge them on the go. Pack spare batteries as additional backups.

Defense

You want a very reliable and sturdy knife for your bug-out bag. It will come in very handy when trying to cut/chop wood for fire or to even harvest plants and crops. It can also be used as a self-defense weapon against animals and other attackers. Make sure that your knife is in a sheath so that you don't harm yourself or others accidentally.

You should always also carry pepper spray because it is a great way to disarm animals and humans without resorting to bloodshed.

Remember that you don't want to kill unless it is absolutely necessary.

Finally, there are always other items that you can use as a weapon in your bug-out bag. Anything can be a weapon. You may be walking and see a large, heavy stick. This in itself can be a suitable weapon for you to use to stun attackers. Always keep your eye out for anything that can be used as a weapon and keep it as close by as possible.

First Aid

Your first aid kit should have the essential items needed for a first aid kit, including additional items like sunscreen. It should also come with first aid instructions, since you may not be familiar with how to use certain items. The checklist below will list all the first aid items you need.

Navigation Tools

A good GPS system, map of the area, and compass are all very good survival items to carry with you. Even if you might think you know the area very well, you can still get lost and stuck, unable to find your way out of an area.

Multi-purpose Tools

Multi-purpose tools can be used to dig, build and secure shelter, chop wood, hunt, fish, create traps, protect yourself, make repairs, break tough things, clear paths, and carry out other actions that you need to survive.

Miscellaneous

Miscellaneous things include radios (to keep in contact with the world around you), walkie-talkies (for communication), copies of important documents, your passport, sewing kits, contact details and addresses of loved ones, goggles (to protect your eyes), ear muffs or ear plugs (to protect your ears) and so on.

Bug-out Bags On a Budget

Even if you are on a tight budget, there are still ways to make a cheap bug-out bag for each member of your family. Remember that there is no need to go out and buy new things if you already have them in your home! Rummage around and see what you can find to save money. This way, you can create your bug-out bag for under $20.

Ensure the bag you purchase is thick, durable, and strong. You don't want the straps to break while you are running from gunfire, for instance. Try to purchase a good one on sale to stay within your budget. Ensure it is water-resistant and air-tight; has padded, thick straps; separated pockets, with many compartments; and roll-top expanded storage.

BUDGET BUG-OUT BAG CHECKLIST

Here is what you should pack in your bug-out bag on a budget:

- Durable backpack
- Alcohol wipes
- Chargeable flashlight
- Snack bars and energy/protein bars
- Band-aids
- Bottle(s) of water
- Pen and notepad
- Cash

- Emergency blanket
- Change of clothes, underwear, and socks
- Toothbrush and toothpaste
- Thick beach towel
- Map of local area
- Dust mask/bandana
- Prescription medication
- Spare prescription glasses
- Alcohol wipes
- Pocket knife
- Chap-Stick
- Soap
- Deodorant
- Work gloves/leather gloves
- Deck of cards, palm-sized games and/or a book
- Charging cable(s)
- Ziplock bags
- USB wall plugs
- Poncho or umbrella
- Durable plastic cup
- Fork and spoon
- Lighter/matches

AN IDEAL CHECKLIST

The items in your bug-out bag may vary slightly based on your specific needs and your location. Nonetheless, the essentials that you need will not change. You may think, for example, that you do not need a warm jacket in a hot climate, but temperatures could fall dramatically at night, leaving you at risk if you cannot protect yourself. Below is an ideal bug-out bag checklist to help you pack, for when SHTF or when disaster strikes.

- Air filtration mask
- Water filtration system
- Water carrying solution
- Emergency food rations
- Sunscreen
- Bandages/band-aids
- Painkillers
- Mini-shovel
- Ax
- Crowbar
- Duct tape
- Foldable saw
- Multi-tool
- Paracord

- Anti-bacterial & antiseptic wipes
- Antibiotic ointment
- First aid kit (with instructions)
- Gauze pads
- Medical gloves
- Burn gel
- Sling
- Tourniquet
- Sleeping bag
- Tent
- Space blanket
- Air filtration mask
- Fishing kit
- Waterproof jacket
- Change of clothes, including underwear and socks
- Cold weather gloves
- Fingerless heavy-duty gloves
- Hand warmers
- Headgear
- Headlamp
- Change of clothes
- Knife
- Pepper spray
- Whistle

- Hand warmers
- Matches, lighter, or other suitable fire starter
- Chemlights
- Flashlights
- Compass
- Maps of your local area
- GPS tracking system
- Charger
- Goggles
- Sewing kit
- Copies of important documents in two USB sticks
- Emergency cash
- Prescription drugs
- Small mirror
- Power source
- Ear muffs/plugs
- Goggles

Although this is an ideal list, it is better to have a more limited bug-out bag than no bag at all. Half a loaf is better than none, meaning that it is better to use what you have now and at least create something that will last you a few days in a worst-case scenario than to have nothing at all.

BUG-OUT PLAN

Along with your bug-out bag, you will also need a bug-out plan. Your bug-out plan is even more important than your bug-out bag because you can survive without a bug-out bag as long as you have a plan. During a disaster, it is very difficult to think about what you need to do and how to do it well to survive. Your body is running on adrenaline and you are not clear of mind. A bug-out plan essentially prevents you from making mistakes but helps you to make the best decisions that ensure survival.

Here are five steps you need to consider when making a bug-out plan:

1. **What kind of disasters are most likely to occur in your area?**

What natural disasters typically occur in your area, such as earthquakes or floods? What other types of disasters have your area suffered from? You can't prepare for every disaster, so knowing the most likely disaster you will face in your area helps you tailor your bug-out plan for the best chance of survival.

2. **What strengths and weaknesses are you working with or against?**

If you are the strongest one in the family, perhaps you will carry the baby if you have to walk long distances. If you have a doctor in the family, they will be in charge of every medical emergency. Your bug-out plan should complement your strengths and prepare for your weaknesses. If you don't know how to read maps and compasses or identify which local plants arc cdiblc or poisonous, your bug-out plan tells you how to do this.

The more skills you gain before disaster strikes, the less you have to carry in your bag. For example, you may not need to carry much food if you know where to find food in your local forest.. For example, you may not need to carry much food if you know where to find food in your local forest.

3. **Plan for specific destinations.**

Where exactly do you want to be when disaster strikes? Also, where do you and your family, friends, neighbors, or any other members of your survival group want to meet? You could all be at separate places when disaster strikes. So deciding where to meet is a great bug-out plan.

Another reason to have a specific location is that you can keep other survival materials there. This also means that you don't have to carry as much in your bug-out bag. It also gives you great peace of mind to know that there is a destination waiting for you: there is a home waiting for you. A positive mindset increases your chances of survival.

Great locations to meet are your relatives' house, your second home or your cabin. You can also meet at large public facilities or local shelters.

4. Plan for four destinations.

Your plan is to get to a safe destination in the event of a disaster. However, your safe destination might not be safe after all. Perhaps it has experienced the same disaster that you have. Or, perhaps, refugees are not being allowed in. It is best to practice having four destinations, at least, as part of your bug-out plan. Make sure that there is a destination on each cardinal direction on the map, i.e. North, South, East, West. This keeps your plans flexible in case of any unforeseen circumstances.

5. Calculate your average travel speed.

How long would it take you to reach your destination? To find this out you will need to calculate your average travel speed. This will let you know how much you can carry with you. You don't want to carry a bug-out bag with all the essentials, only to find that you cannot carry it after a certain time because it is too heavy. Typically, you will only be able to carry a bag that weighs 25% of your weight. You will carry your bag for hours and days. Ensure it is not too heavy.

Usually, the average person can walk 2.5-4 miles per hour on flat terrain. If there are children, pets, or vulnerable people in your party, this will take, at least, twice as long. Additionally, the terrain in your local area will give you an idea of how fast you can walk. If it is downhill or uphill, you, of course, will need more time than average.

Get Home Bag

Any good prepper in the know has a get-home bag (GHB). Your get-home bag, as the name suggests, helps you get home after a disaster. Your goal is to get home as quickly as possible. Perhaps you were at work when disaster struck and need to get home to pick up your kids and your bug-out bag. Or perhaps you need to get home to pick up your pets.

You use a get-home bag when you are not too far away from home. Obviously, you will not choose to use a get home back if you were in Australia and your home is in Alaska. As a result, your GBH should be light and keep you alive for no more than a couple of days. You need to pack only the very basic essentials, like a water bottle and water filter, and food to keep you going, such as trail mix and energy bars. You may also pack a few other tool basics, such as a multi-tool, duct tape, and a first aid kit. Keep your GHB where you spend the most time outside of the home. This would be in your workplace or in your car. For children, this will be in their lockers at school.

SURVIVAL TASK

Think about the five most important items that you will need in your bug-out bag. This could be important medication, contact details, prescription glasses, and so many other items. Make sure these five items can meet your personal needs. The aim is to personalize your bug-out bag to your own needs, too. Your five items should also be items found in at least one checklist in this book.

Key Chapter Takeaway

- Refresh your bug-out bag periodically, ensuring it contains all you need to survive in a life-or-death scenario.
- Bug-out bags are not just for venturing out into the wild. They are also for surviving at home.
- A bug-out bag is always ready for use in case of an emergency.

- The items in your bug-out bag may vary slightly based on your specific needs and your location.
- Your bug-out bag must be created based on the survival rule of 3. The survival rule of 3 states that there are 3 things that you cannot survive without food, water, and air.
- It is better to have a more limited bug-out bag than no bag at all.
- Your bug-out plan is even more important than your bug-out bag because you can survive without a bug-out bag as long as you have a plan.

In the next chapter, you will learn how to store an emergency supply of water, how to purify water, and how to find a source of water once those supplies have run out.

Chapter Three: Hydration Is Key

You can go 3 days without water before you die. This doesn't seem like a big deal when you have running water coming out of every faucet in your house, but life can be very precarious, as are the systems and infrastructure we have in place to keep us alive. All it takes is one storm or one burst pipe and you could suddenly find yourself without water to drink or with only contaminated water available. Once that happens, the clock is ticking down for you and your family.

For many non-preppers, this will be a difficult life-or-death situation. For you, this will be another challenge you wisely prepped for. The cold, hard fact of life is that being thirsty is a horrible feeling. Our ancestors knew this, and that is why they always stored clean, drinkable, non-contaminated water.

Like our ancestors, your goal is to keep even more water than you need to increase your chances of survival. As any good prepper would surmise, hydration is, indeed, key. To prep you for staying hydrated during a disaster, remember the framework, W.A.S.P.S.

- **W**hen in doubt, double your ration.
- **A**lways drink now and worry about later.
- **S**anitize containers to stay alive.
- **P**urify your water without fail.
- **S**ource your water from many sources!

We have become too used to having running water, but it takes just one disaster to snap us out of our spoiled state. As a serious prepper, here are the water facts you need to memorize to face disaster head-on:

- How much do you need to store?
- How to store it.
- How to source clean water.
- How to purify water.

How Much Water Should I Store?

The standard storage unit for water is one gallon per day per person. Usually, a regularly active person will need to drink about half a gallon of water daily, but doubling it errs on the side of caution. You will need water not just for drinking but also for cooking and cleaning, so you will need to double it if you plan to do more than drinking it. Remember, when in doubt, double your ration.

How much water you decide to store depends on your needs. Do you plan to be on the move? In that case, you cannot carry with you 30 gallons of water. A water purifier on the go would be your best choice. However, if you plan to survive in a bunker or another such location, then storing as much water as your storage would allow is a good idea. You will also need to think about where/how to store water, as will be discussed later in this chapter.

No matter what happens, do not ration water. Always drink now and worry about water later. Drink however much water you need to survive for the day and then try to find more water the next day. Rationing water is like trying to ration oxygen—it just won't work. You can try to reduce your need for water, however, by keeping cool and reducing your level of activity. Keep in mind the survival rule of 3. You need food, water, and air. Water and air are the topmost important priority for any human. No other need can be fulfilled unless those two are prioritized.

How To Store Water

The number one rule for storing water is to store it in a cool, dry place, e.g. a pantry or a basement. This will prevent bacteria and other microorganisms from growing and contaminating your water. The easiest way to store water is in a reusable container with a lid and one that is easy to carry. This makes empty water bottles, bricks, canisters, and barrels a great resource for storing water. To save on space, you can purchase collapsible bottles and canisters that take up less space when empty and are easy to carry while on the move.

Pre-bottled water will typically last 2-5 years if left unopened, making it a great way to store water. It is also affordable, portable, easy to carry, and widely available. Bigger storage containers, like 5-gallon water containers, are an alternative water storage method for storing larger quantities of water. You can also purchase 55-gallon water barrels for your bug-out shelter. If used well, a barrel can last one person for a month. If you want to store even more water in one go (following the framework of doubling your ration), purchase 160-gallon water storage tanks or a Water Bob, which is a device that allows you to fill up your tub with water without contaminating the water with your well-used tub.

You will need to replace your pre-bottled water once it expires, to prevent contamination. For alternative water storage options, use food-grade, non-degradable, sanitized, airtight containers that have never been used to store a hazardous substance. In a pinch, you can also use other containers in your home, as long as you sanitize them and they have not been previously used to store hazardous materials.

How to Source Water

It might seem like the pressure to source water is enormous, but there are always options, unless, of course, you decide to bug out in the Sahara desert. Even then, there are oases in the desert for sourcing water. There will always be a source of water. Simply put, your chances of survival increase the more sources you use. That way, when one method fails (whether temporarily or permanently) there is another to keep you alive.

Your three primary sources of emergency water supply are:

1. **Emergency water sources inside your home.**

There are some excellent sources of emergency water in your home. They are:

Ice

If you have a freezer, then you have ice. You never know when your electricity will go out or come back on during a disaster, so it is a good idea to empty your freezer (and fridge) as quickly as possible. Otherwise, you might find yourself looking at spoiled food, as well as a defrosted freezer making a messy puddle around your kitchen.

To collect ice from your freezer, simply scrape the ice into a bowl and allow it to defrost for a few minutes or hours. If you don't need to use the ice right away, you can put the bowl back into the freezer, still containing the ice. That way it can continue to keep your food preserved for at least a few hours until you're ready to use the ice or eat the food.

Shelf-Stable Beverages

Shelf stable beverages are beverages that can last a long time when left unopened. Things like fruit juices and cartons of milk are significant sources of water since they contain nutrients and electrolytes that your body desperately needs. You will of course still need to drink water, however, they can act as a short-term replacement once or twice a day.

Don't be fooled into thinking that carbonated beverages can be a great water replacement source. Along with alcoholic beverages and caffeinated drinks, they actually deplete your body of water, leaving you even more dehydrated than if you have not drunk them in the first place. You certainly don't want to be dehydrated in a disaster scenario because it can quickly turn dangerous if you cannot find water on time.

Household Pipes

Even after the main water supply is turned off in your home, there is still water stored in the pipes. You can't turn on the taps to get the water, so you will need to use gravity. To do this, you need to turn on the lowest level faucet in your house to the highest level. This pumps air into your plumbing and causes a steady drip of water to trickle out. Since it is normal water from your pipes, it is drinkable for the next few days.

Hot Water Heater/Tank

Hot water heaters/tanks are like your pipes. They always have water stored in them. Depending on the hot water heater you have, it will have between 20-50 gallons of water stored in it. This water is, of course, the same as the water in your pipes, which is then fed into your water heater. So this means that it is clean and drinkable. Make sure you shut off the main water valve immediately before or after a disaster (whichever you can manage) to prevent contamination.

We've already mentioned water heaters are all very different. As is the creed of every prepper, you must be prepared. In the case of your water heater, this means knowing what type and grade of water heater you have.

Become familiar with it to understand its design and how it works. Unlike a non-prepper, you will be prepared with all the information and tools you need to work your water heater efficiently when disaster strikes. Frankly, it is impossible to read a water heater manual when a tornado is approaching, for example. To get the water stored in your hot water tank/heater, follow the instructions below:

1. Read your hot water tank manual to familiarize yourself with how your tank works.

2. Turn off the electric or gas supply to your hot water heater. If it is a natural gas heater, you will need to turn the handle perpendicular to the pipe to turn it off.

3. Turn off the water intake valve located at the top of your water heater. Turning it off will protect the water stored in your heater from contamination.

4. Find the pressure and temperature relief valve found either at the top or side of your tank.

5. Protect the water in the tank from outside contamination by turning off the water intake valve at the top of the tank. This will allow the water to flow by breaking suction. You will not need to shut off your intake valve or power source if you are only planning on collecting a few gallons of water as part of your regular practice.

6. Use a handy tool, such as a screwdriver, to turn on the drain valve faucet. The drain valve faucet is located at the

bottom of the tank/heater. Use a clean, non-contaminated container to collect the water.

7. You and everyone else in your survival party should follow these steps to practice draining water from your hot water tank regularly. The good news is that draining water from your tank regularly will prolong the life of your water heater by removing sediment and particles that build up at the bottom.

You can already see that there are good places inside your home to find emergency water sources. As a prepper, being able to see things that other non-preppers cannot see is what distinguishes you from those who may not survive. This is an impressive skill to develop because, no matter where you find yourself during a disaster, you need to be able to spot emergency water sources to survive.

2. Emergency water sources around your home.

Just like emergency water sources inside your home, there are many sources of emergency water around your home. Some of the best ones are:

Rainwater

Did you know that in many countries today rainwater is still collected as a source of free clean water? And why not? Rainwater has always been collected by humans because it is nature's way of providing us with good, uncontaminated water.

Depending on where you are in the world collecting rainwater might be illegal so, we would recommend that you look up laws in your area and country. During a disaster, you won't be prosecuted for collecting rainwater to survive.

You can create your own makeshift rainwater catchment system using your rain gutters and a clean rain barrel. If you don't have a rain barrel, a clean large container or bucket will also work fine. Rainwater is generally clean unless it comes into contact with a dirty surface or with the ground. If this occurs, filter and purify your water with the methods described in this chapter.

Swimming Pool

Swimming pool water may not seem like an obvious choice of clean water, especially for drinking, however it is entirely doable if the water is treated and has not been swum in. Don't drink it, but it is still an excellent source of hygienic water, for example, water for taking a shower or cleaning your home.

You will need, however, to filter your swimming pool water as it will contain chemicals such as chlorine. By distilling the water, you make it safe to drink and use. Distilling the water basically removes all the impurities and chemicals from it. You might be tempted to think that boiling swimming water is good enough to make it clean and pure, however, this will not remove chemicals already in the water. You can harm yourself if you drink boiled swimming pool water, so be careful!

The Big Berkey Water Filter (described below) is great for distilling swimming pool water and claims to remove 99.9% of heavy metals and up to 99.9% of chlorine in swimming pool water (Berkey Filters, 2022). Note, however, that they advise you to only use it in emergencies because it significantly decreases the number of uses left on your filter once you filter out swimming pool water (Berkey Filters, 2022). You also have the option to use AquaRain filters to purify swimming pool water. The one downside to these filters is that they do not remove salt or any naturally occurring minerals from the water. Conversely, they are very handy because all you need to do is add AquaRain into a 5-gallon bucket of swimming pool water and it filters it for you!

If you want to use any other brands of filters, that is perfectly fine. You just need to ensure that you do proper research first. Many filter brands may claim to filter and purify water perfectly, but they may not filter out chlorine, salt, minerals, or any other chemicals. It is always a good bet to invest in the more expensive filters because they are more effective.

Plant Transpiration

This method of collecting water will only get you about half a cup of water in five hours. It is not a very effective method of collecting water in general disaster scenarios, but it is a great method for serious emergencies when you have no other alternatives. When plants transpire, they release vapor through their pores. You can collect this water for drinking purposes.

To do so, wrap a clean and sanitized plastic bag around the branch of a living bush or tree. Make sure the branch is in direct sunlight and the plastic bag is not wrapped too tightly. It should have enough space to collect between ⅓ to ½ cup of water. Leave the plastic bag for about 4 to 5 hours, allowing the plant to transpire and release vapor, which the bag will then collect.

Before a disaster occurs, do your research on which plants are toxic. That way, you do not collect toxic water that could cause serious harm to your health. You also have to keep with you, at all times, clean plastic bags that you can use to collect water through transpiration. Memorize how this method works because it is a great emergency water supply while bugging out.

Below-Ground Solar Still

A below-ground solar still uses the same method of collecting water as plant transpiration. How does it work?

Get a clean, sanitized bowl and dig a hole in the ground just big enough to fit this bowl and hold your plant. Make sure the hole is in an area that receives plenty of sunlight for hours at a time. Build a reservoir inside the pit just big enough to hold your bowl, then place your non-toxic plant in the pit.

Use a sheet of clear sanitized plastic to cover the pit and then secure the edges well so that the plastic does not move. You can place stones or other heavy objects around the edges to do this. Then, create an indent in the center of the plastic by placing a rock or slightly heavy object just on top of the position of the bowl in the pit. Don't use an object that is too heavy because it will break the sheet. As the plant transpires, the condensation will rise and build up on the plastic sheet. The indent in the sheet will work with gravity to pull the water downwards into the bowl at the bottom of the pit.

Water Generating Units

A water-generating unit can be used as a backup source of water. Why is it only a backup source of water? Well, it only works with electricity. That means that you cannot use it if the power goes out during a disaster. Nonetheless, following the framework, "source your water from many sources", having one as a backup is never a bad idea!

A water generating unit works by harvesting water in the air and converting it into drinkable water. It works best if you live in a hot and humid climate where there is plenty of condensed moisture in the air to harvest.

3. Emergency water sources from surrounding areas.

Luckily, when a disaster occurs, there are always people around to help. Disaster does not stop every resource from the area from working at the same time, so you will be able to find other sources of water in your surroundings. Simply make sure that the water that you collect from surrounding areas is from clean, uncontaminated sources. Do your due diligence. Ask questions and inspect the sources if you can. Then, filter the water after it is collected.

Some significant sources of emergency water from surrounding areas are:

Local Bodies of Water

There are different types of bodies of water and some are better than others. Flowing water, like rivers, is always better than stagnant water, like lakes. However, the best local body of water source is spring water from an underground source. They are usually the safest water for drinking. Rivers and flowing streams are also often good sources of clean water. You always have to consider the source of the water, as we've already discussed. What is in the surroundings of the underground source of your spring water? What is upstream of your flowing stream or river? This does not mean that you should not filter all sources of water from local bodies even if the source is clean. There are so many ways for pollutants, waste, pesticides, fertilizers, and many other poisonous chemicals to get into local bodies of water, so always take precaution. Remember to always "purify your water without fail."

Stagnant water such as lakes and ponds, on the other hand, is more likely to be contaminated with pollutants. Floodwaters, marshes and swamp water are all severely contaminated and should be avoided even in severe emergencies, unless you have the Big Berkey Water Filter.

Private Well Water

If you or someone in your surrounding area has a well, then this is another good source of emergency water for you. Be cautious because well water can be polluted or contaminated, for example, if a dead animal has fallen into it. Follow the hydration framework and purify it before using.

You will also need a way to get the water out of the well. If the well is not too deep, you can use a hand crank and bucket or a rope tied to a small bucket to get water out. This is a very labor-intensive process, so a pump might be more suitable. While electric pumps are handy, non-electric ones will work even when the electricity is out. There are also solar-powered pumps that you can invest in now if you do indeed have access to a well. While it might seem frivolous to spend money on a solar-powered pump now, it could be a lifesaver when the chips are down. Last, if you have a back-up generator and some fuel, you can use this to pump water.

Water From Government or Humanitarian Agencies

After a disaster, relief efforts are always organized to get to survivors and those in need. Clean, drinkable water is one of the first supplies sent, so chances are that you will receive water from the government and other humanitarian agencies.

Yes, this is always good as a back-up plan, but it is not advisable to rely on this source of water. You will have to stand in line for hours with very cranky, hungry, tired, and desperate people. Things can go south very quickly in such an environment, hence being self-reliant for water is a better choice after all.

WATER PURIFICATION

Even if you're not able to store water, it is imperative that you're able to purify water. If you don't have any stored water, as long as you're able to purify your water, you can go out searching for a source of water. Additionally, in case of emergencies when you need to be on the move, you won't be able to carry water with you because it is very heavy.

A purifier is a perfect in-between option. It is light enough to carry and still provides you with clean water. The only difference is you will need to then source water. Luckily, there are different methods for purifying water depending on which works best for you.

1. **Boiling water**

Boiling water is the most traditional way of purifying water. Simply boil for ten minutes to allow enough time to kill all the dangerous microorganisms.

2. Iodine

You can use iodine tincture from a first aid kit to purify water if you have no other options. You will need to prep it first: Let it sit for 30 minutes if it's warm outside and an hour if it's hot. Add ten drops per gallon. Don't use too much, otherwise, it can be poisonous.

3. Rocks, sand, and charcoal

This method of purification reduces the bacteria in water and makes it better, although it will not protect you from Giardia. To purify, layer a clean sock (or any other straining container) with sand placed at the bottom. Layer charcoal on the sand then add rocks lastly. Filter your water into a container.

4. Chlorination

Chlorination kills most microorganisms in water. To chlorinate water, there are three methods that you can use. They are:

Chlorine dioxide tablets and water drops

This works by simply dropping the chlorine dioxide tablets into your water and letting the tablets do their job. The tablets treat the water with chemicals that are safe to ingest, killing all the disease-causing microorganisms in the water. You can use portable tablets which work effectively well against bacteria, viruses, Lamblia, Giardia, and Cryptosporidium. You may also use water drops. Ensure that the water drops you choose are EPA-registered. Water drops can chlorinate gallons of water in one go since they are essentially chlorine dioxide tablets in liquid form.

Chlorine bleach

Like chlorine dioxide water drops, chlorine blcach can treat gallons of water in one go with just a little amount. If you decide to use chlorine bleach, you will need to shake the water and then wait for 30 minutes before using it. At the same time, be aware that chlorine bleach does not kill Giardia, as chlorine tablets or drops do. However, it will prevent cholera.

Using bleach to purify water typically follows more rules than using tablets or drops.

First, avoid scented bleaches, bleaches with added cleaners or color-safe bleaches. These types of bleaches are toxic for you and your family, thanks to the added chemicals! They will only contaminate your water. If the bleach contains any types of dyes, perfumes, or other additives, then skip it!

Second, use bleach specifically designed for drinking water and not pool water. Chlorine bleach designed for pool water is a different chemical compound altogether and is a corrosive pesticide. Not only will your water taste bad, but it will also be too toxic for ingestion.

Third, be aware that chlorine bleach is effective for only six months after it is manufactured, so you will need to rotate it often, as well as ensure that you are not using expired bleach.

The simple fact is that bleach is not meant for human consumption. We recommend you keep it only for emergency usage. Why? Well, bleach is carcinogenic. When you add bleach to your water, it oxidizes any organic contaminants living in the water. This process produces trihalomethanes, which are famous for causing cancer.

It is also very important that you follow the instructions on the warning very closely. If you add too much bleach into your water, it will become extremely poisonous and corrosive, also damaging anything it comes in contact with, including your skin, organs, and other body parts.

Therefore, think of bleach as only a short-term option to tide you over until you can find other sources of purifying your water during a disaster.

5. Filtration

Filtering water is a great way to purify it of all disease-causing parasites and any other contaminants. We recommend three different water filters:

Lifestraw Water Filter

As its name suggests, Lifestraw water filter works like a drinking straw that filters water as you drink. It is a lightweight and portable option that filters out 99.9999% of waterborne protozoan parasites and bacteria. It is a great option to place in your bug-out bag for when you are on the move.

Katadyn Water Filter

Used by the military, the Katadyn water filter is a very durable and long-lasting option for filtering up to 13,000 gallons of water with an output of about 1 quart or 1 liter per minute.

Big Berkey Water Filter

The Big Berkey water filter can filter up to 3,000 gallons of water. It is great for everyday use since it is portable, has a long filter life, and can filter not just treated water, but untreated water from stagnant and flowing bodies of water, such as lakes, ponds, and streams.

SURVIVAL TASK

Think where you could store water on your property. What systems do you have in place to purify water? Where is your closest natural water source?

Create a mini-plan containing the information you'll need should water sourcing become a problem during an emergency.

Key Chapter Takeaway

- The standard storage unit for water is one gallon per day per person. You will need to double this to factor in using water for hygiene.
- How much water you decide to store depends on your needs. Will you be on the move or will you be planning on bugging out or bugging in?
- Never ration water. Always drink now and worry about water later.
- Store water in a cool, dry place, preferably with a lid on.
- Pre-bottled bottles of water, bricks, canisters, and barrels are a great resource for storing water.

- Pre-bottled water will typically last 2-5 years if left unopened, making it a great way to store water.
- Replace your pre-bottled water once they expire, to prevent contamination.
- Water storage: use food-grade, non-degradable, sanitized, airtight containers that have never been used to store a hazardous substance.
- There are sources of emergency water in and around your home and in your surrounding area.
- If you're not able to store water, you must be able to purify water. That way, you can go out searching for a source of water.
- Water purifiers help you purify water when you are bugging out.
- There are different methods for purifying water depending on which works best for your situation.

In the next chapter, you will learn the different ways you can store food for emergencies, including the different ways you can become more self-sufficient when thinking long-term about food resources.

Chapter Four: Calories Are Good!

In an emergency, calories are good. Most of us spend every waking minute counting our calories because we want to eat fewer calories. Ironically, during a disaster, the opposite is true: you want to consume as many calories as you possibly can to stay alive. It is simple human biology: when food is plentiful; you try to eat less. And when food is scarce, you spend your energy and time trying to eat as much as you can.

During a disaster, your nervous system is also working overtime to keep you grounded despite being in a very stressful situation. As a result, your body will seriously rely on calories to keep you working at your most efficient level. Hence, calories become massively important when trying to survive during a disaster.

This chapter aims to explore the different ways that you can store food for emergencies, how much food you should have ready, and also ways you can become more self-sufficient when thinking long-term about food resources.

Yes, you want to store as many calories as you can, but you also want to store them well. Avoiding food contamination and spoilage is just as important as storing the food in the first place. There is just no point going through all of that effort and time, and spending all of that money, stockpiling food, only to have it go to waste because you did not store it properly.

Four types of food contamination can leave you severely sick and even lead to death. They are:

Microbial

Microbial contamination occurs when living microbes in the air contaminate your food. Microbes, such as viruses, fungi, bacteria, mold, and toxins, are toxic to humans. Indeed, microbial contamination is one of the most common causes of food contamination, as well as food poisoning, for humans.

The simple fact is that microbes are everywhere, so you have to take very careful precautions to avoid food contamination. The first thing you must do is ensure that you prepare all your food properly, especially highly contaminable foods like raw chicken and fish. Never eat highly contaminable foods that are not cooked thoroughly, no matter how hungry you are. It is best to stay hungry and forage for food the next day than to eat food that will leave you dead in the next few days.

Another way to prevent microbial contamination is to store and prepare foods that are risky away from other foods. Keep them very separate from your other foods and wash and disinfect all surfaces that they touch as soon as preparation is completed. In fact, clean and disinfect all surfaces in your bug-out residence regularly. This may be difficult when there is not much water, so store bottles of antibacterial spray as a precaution.

Always wash raw fruits and vegetables and take very good care of your hygiene. Wash or disinfect your hands regularly, take regular showers and wash your hair often.

Do not leave out open containers of raw or cooked food at any point because it attracts microbes. Microbes also love moist, humid conditions, so take care to prevent this wherever you store your food. Open windows when it is hot and close them when it is cold and/or humid. Finally, keep all your food in moisture-proof and air-proof containers.

Physical

This physical contamination is any physical object that contaminates your food during the food preparation or storing process. Anything counts as a physical contaminant, including hair, broken glass, stones, fingernails, toys, bits of plastic, jewelry, pests–anything really. Not only can physical contamination cause things like choking or broken teeth, it can also carry microbes that end up causing food poisoning.

You can prevent physical food contamination by keeping all your foods in tight and sealed containers. Don't use damaged cooking or food storage equipment that can break into your food, remove all jewelry and pull back your hair before cooking. Last, cultivate an environment that is unfriendly to pests. Keep your food storage and preparation area clean and dry at all times and keep it at cool temperatures to dissuade pests. Make sure there are no openings for pests to enter your food storage areas, such as windows and chimneys, and fumigate regularly. To cultivate an area unfriendly to pests, never leave cooked or raw food out for even short periods. The smell alone is enough to attract them.

Allergenic

We all know what allergies are and we all know how serious they can get. Even if no one in your survival party is allergic to anything, don't forget that allergies can start at any time in a person's life, so always store allergenic-free food, just in case.

If there is a person with allergies in your survival party, then you must always keep allergenic food separate from all your other food and avoid using the same kitchen utensils, preparation area, and clothes for all these. Clean and disinfect your kitchen often, as we've already discussed, and stick to food that comes from suppliers who take allergenic contamination seriously.

There are 14 major food allergies. They are:

1. Milk
2. Eggs
3. Celery and celeriac (found in stock cubes, ready meals, spice mixes, sauces, and savory flavorings)
4. Fish
5. Sesame seeds
6. Crustacean shellfish
7. Tree nuts
8. Sulfur dioxide and sulfite (found in dehydrated vegetables, dried fruit, pickled foods, processed meats, and salad dressings)
9. Peanuts
10. Mustard
11. Wheat
12. Lupin
13. Soybeans

14. Mollusk (mussels, clams, oysters, and oyster sauce)

Chemical

Although you might strive to keep your food preparation and storage area as clean as possible, the chemicals that you use, for example, antibacterial spray or fumigation chemicals, could end up contaminating your food as well. Even before purchase, your food may also be sprayed with fertilizers and pesticides that are not good for human consumption. So, always keep all your food completely covered while cleaning the area and wash your food thoroughly before cooking or preparing.

Now that you know how to store food, this chapter will take you through where to store food, how to create your foods to create your food storage checklist, and how to preserve your own food.

But, first, there is a framework to help you remember how to manage your relationship with food during a disaster:

- **G**row your own.
- **A**lways store well.
- **P**reserve your own.
- **S**tore plenty.

Where To Store Food

Remember that you are storing plenty. Calories are very good in a survival situation! You never know when your food will run out, so don't take chances. Store as much as you can; use every space available to you!

Sometimes it's difficult to pinpoint places to store your food—especially if you are not a seasoned prepper. To help you along, here is a list of potential places to store your food:

Basement Storage Room

A cool, dark basement is a great place to store your food. The ideal condition for storing food is in cool, dark spaces. If your basement typically gets too hot or cold, then it is not a great place to store your food. You can build shelves in your basement to give you more space for storing your food.

Food Storage Closet

Closets in your house will often have extra space to store some food. Even just placing a box filled with cans in your clothes closet will work. You should also be able to find space in your closets to add shelves and create more space for food storage.

Over the Door Shelf Storage

This works just like a food storage closet. If there is a space over your wall, you can hang a couple of shelves to hold your food. It may not be a good idea, however, if you live in a place that's prone to earthquakes or other natural disasters.

Under the Bed Storage

You can place food in storage boxes under your bed. Simply ensure that you do not choose food in breakable containers, like glass jars, to avoid accidents.

Storage Furniture

Use furniture that comes with storage. Sofas, coffee tables and most furniture can come with adequate storage space. If you have an empty wall, then you can also place a storage cabinet there to store extra food.

Laundry Room Storage

Just like over-the-door storage, you can place shelves in strategic positions in your laundry room, for example, above your washer and dryer. Laundry rooms rarely have windows. So, you will need to consider how to provide adequate ventilation to prevent your food from spoiling.

Under the Stairs

If you have space under your stairs, you can turn it into a storage closet. You will need to consider how to provide adequate ventilation when storing food under the stairs.

Trailers, Campers, and Boats

Trailers, stored campers, and boats will store your food well, although only for a short time.

Thanks to temperature fluctuations, they do not provide ideal conditions for long-term food storage. You will need to rotate the food frequently. The one good advantage of storing food in your camper is that you can evacuate quickly in the case of an emergency.

Garage and Shed Storage

The good news is that, if you have a garage or shed, you can put up plenty of shelves to store your food. The bad news is that if your garage or shed does not have temperature control, your food will go bad very quickly thanks to temperature fluctuations. We prefer to think of garages and sheds as short-term storage solutions. Since your food will go bad quickly, it is best to use the food stored in your garage or shed first during a disaster. You will also need to rotate supplies in your garage/shed fairly regularly.

Root Cellars and Crawl Spaces

Root cellars and crawl spaces are another short-term storage solution. They have very humid air, so you will need to rotate your food regularly. Protect your food in moisture-proof plastic bags or containers

Buried Chest Freezer

Buried chest freezers and water-tight barrels are a great way to store your fruit and vegetables over the winter. They are also good for storing canned and jarred foods, as long as you use good quality, moisture-proof and rodent-proof barrels, and freezers.

Suitcases

Fill empty suitcases with food supplies and leave them in a cool, dry place.

STARTER FOOD STORAGE CHECKLIST

Here is a list of all the food that we recommend you have stored in your home for emergencies. This is just a guide. You can adapt this as you require, but this is a great starting point as this will be enough for a family to survive for months until you can find an alternative source of food.

1. 20lbs of rice

Rice is a must-have. If you want a quick source of carbs and calories, then rice is your best friend. It is versatile, so it is difficult to run out of recipes using rice. It is also very filling and nutritious.

We recommend you store a combination of white rice and brown rice. White rice is easier and faster to cook and it lasts longer when stored. Brown rice, on the other hand, has much more fiber, which keeps up your health in an emergency. It is also more filling and nutritious than white rice. Be aware, however, that brown rice will not last longer than a few months.

On the plus side, you have other options of rice, such as Basmati (brown and white), sticky rice, jasmine rice, wild rice, and more.

2. 20lbs of dried beans

Dried beans are another versatile source of food. Whether Pinto Beans, kidney beans, or any other form of beans, dried beans store for a long time, are nutritious, inexpensive, and can be used to create many recipes. They are also incredibly tasty and don't need many ingredients to taste delicious.

3. 20 cans of fruit

You need your micronutrients. Luckily, fruit contains many essential vitamins and minerals. Store pineapples, peaches, strawberries, pears, fruit cocktails, and whatever other fruits you desire. Fruits are also a great source of quick energy and a healthy form of dessert to boost your spirits in an emergency.

4. 20 cans of vegetables

Store as many vegetables as you can. That way, you get a full spectrum of micronutrients. You can store peas, corn, mixed fruit, asparagus, tomatoes, green beans, and so much more. We recommend you store an additional 20 cans of tomatoes because tomatoes are so versatile and can be used to make many dishes, including dishes made from rice and/or beans.

5. 20 cans of meat

You will need your iron and protein. Meat and fish are a great source of all three, so stock up on canned beef, spam, tuna, chicken, salmon, sausages, shrimp, etc...

A vegetarian diet is the most practical diet in emergency situations. However, there are times your body will still need meat/fish, especially since you are under the stress of surviving in a disaster scenario.

6. 4lbs oats

Oats are another versatile survival essential. They are packed with carbs and protein, so they fill you up for a long time, giving you the energy you need to survive a disaster/emergency. They are also versatile, with their ability to make many recipes, using only a few simple ingredients.

7. 5lbs salt

Your body needs salt to survive. It is imperative for many bodily functions and processes, so you must store enough salt to stay healthy.

8. 3 large jars of Peanut Butter

Peanut butter contains plenty of energy and nutritious fat for sustenance. It is also a source of protein and it lasts a long time on the shelf (one year) when unopened. It can also last for about two months when opened.

9. 5lbs powdered milk

You may not be able to find fresh milk during a disaster. In fact, fresh milk can become very rare to source during a disaster because of its brief shelf life. Powdered milk is, therefore, a great substitute. It is full of protein and fat, as well as other nutrients. to sustain you and keep you full. It is also a great addition to your foods and drinks, such as oatmeal, cereal, and coffee.

10. 5lbs coffee and/or 100 tea bags

The exact amount of coffee and tea bags you should buy depends on how much you drink. The coffee and tea bags also depend on what you like.

Stock up on what you like. The familiarity of your favorite flavored coffee or fruit tea bag will bring you a lot of comfort.

11. 10lbs of pasta

It is easy to find and stock pasta. Pasta is easy and fast to cook and very filling. Since it is so versatile to cook, you also won't get bored eating pasta.

12. 10 jars/cans of spaghetti/pasta sauce

On days when you are too tired to cook, or when you may not have enough energy, spaghetti sauce can be warmed up in 10 minutes to go with your pasta.

13. 20 cans of broth or soup

Soup works well for every meal. You don't need to add anything else. Simply warm it for a few minutes and you are set! You can also use it to add flavor to other meals such as rice and pasta dishes.

14. 2 large jars of powdered drink fortified with vitamin C (or an 8 lb bucket of ascorbic acid)

You need your vitamin C. Unfortunately, vitamin C is found in fresh fruits and vegetables. You can store juices, but they don't last very long unopened. It would take a lot of canned fruits and vegetables to get the recommended amount of vitamin C, therefore, a powdered drink fortified with vitamin C is your best substitute.

You can also store four jars of concentrated lemon juice. Not only is this a significant source of vitamin C, but it is also a good way of adding flavor to your food during a disaster.

Alternatively, you can purchase ascorbic acid. Our bodies cannot produce vitamin C, so you must get it from an outside source. Still, vitamin C is very important for preventing illnesses and keeping your immune system strong when you are at your most vulnerable (when you are highly stressed).

Ascorbic acid is the best form of vitamin C because it can last a long time without degrading. It is not sensitive to heat like vitamin supplements are and it can also be used during food preservation to minimize oxidation, browning, and discoloration of food.

15. 10lbs of pancake mix

When you are hungry and need something to fill you up for a long time, pancake mix will save the day. You can store a few tubs of margarine and bottles of honey to add as a nice topping. You can also use pancake mix to make crepes, which you can serve with some canned fruit.

16. 2 lbs of honey

Honey is great for strengthening the immune system, helping you to stave off coughs and colds. It will also boost your energy levels—just add a teaspoon to hot water or tea. Honey is a natural antibacterial so it can prevent infection in minor cuts and grazes.

Raw honey works best if you can get it, but this must not be given to infants.

17. 2 large jars of jam

Jam lasts a long time even after it is opened. It is a perfect food for when you need some sweetness and will go with your crepes, pancakes, or bread.

18. One extra large jug of cooking oil

You need oil for cooking. You also need the fat present in the oil to sustain your mind and body. Also, you need to eat fat to enable your body to break down and absorb fat-soluble vitamins and nutrients. You don't need too much oil when cooking. A dash of olive oil, coconut oil, or canola oil is enough to give you that satisfying feeling that oil provides. Plus, the oil adds flavor to your dishes.

19. Herbs, spices, and condiments

You don't want to eat the same food every day because it will get boring. Herbs, spices, and condiments are a great way to change the taste of your food, even if you are cooking the same thing. Buy those that you particularly enjoy. Buy those that go well with most dishes, such as garlic, chili, hot sauce, thyme, black pepper, paprika, oregano, rosemary, bay leaves, and salsa.

20. 2 large bags of hard candies

You want to stay healthy even in survival mode. This means that you do not want to eat too much sugar. However, you also need a good pick-me-up once in a while. Hard candies like lemon drops and butterscotch drops are a great way to find comfort occasionally.

You will notice that all the food on this list is very easy and practical to store and cook. While a beef wellington might sound good, it will require a lot of energy to preserve and prepare. Its aroma will also be too conspicuous, placing you in danger of theft in the process. Your best chance of survival is to store practical, simple food that can be easily combined into fresh meals with little cooking experience.

Other Foods To Provide

You also want to store other calorie-dense foods that can last you a long time. You mustn't store any food that requires specialized tools to either prepare or preserve. They should be easy to cook, last for years, and be packed with nutrients your body needs.

Below is a good list of such foods:

1. Grains

Grains, such as rye, corn, barley, wheat, and spelt can be stored as long as they have less than 10 percent moisture. You can prepare most grains by soaking and cooking them.

Wheat can be stored for as long as 25 to 30 years. Using simple, traditional methods, you can bake bread using just wheat, salt, and water. You can also create your own wood fire oven as will be discussed in the next chapter. There are different varieties of wheat available to you, including gluten-free options such as einkorn.

Plan to store about 300lbs-400lbs of grain per person. If you can purchase a small grain mill, do so. It enables you to grind wheat and grains to use to make tortillas and bread. It also makes your home look like a traditional farmstead, which is a great additional benefit.

2. Potato flakes

Potato flakes are quick to prepare in just a few minutes. All you need is boiling water. They are also a great way to thicken your stews and soups and make them more calorie-dense.

Even better, they contain a high number of micronutrients that your body needs to survive.

3. **Dehydrated and Freeze-Dried vegetables**

It is a no-brainer why you need dehydrated and freeze-dried vegetables. They are packed with nutrients and fiber and they add taste to your food. Onions, carrots, and celery are the most important dried vegetables you need. Onions and celery, in particular, add a lot of flavor to your food, while carrots are a rare source of vitamin A for preppers.

4. **White sugar**

As we've already discussed, you don't want to eat too much sugar as a survivalist. It is not only bad for your overall health but your oral health as well during a time when you may not find a dentist. Nonetheless, sugar is a great preservative. In the next part of this chapter, we will talk about the different ways to preserve food, one of which is sugar. Store about 70lbs of sugar per person.

5. Baking Soda

Baking soda is a wonderfully versatile food product. You can use it for cooking, baking, cleaning, personal hygiene, and medicinal uses. This cheap powder with an infinite shelf-life is a must-have for your survival kitchen. Store 10lbs of baking soda per person.

6. Vinegar

Like baking soda, vinegar has a lot of uses for both cooking and non-cooking. It is used in many recipes and for preserving food by pickling and acidifying. It has great medicinal uses, such as relieving indigestion, and is a brilliant disinfectant and cleaner.

There are a variety of kinds of vinegar available to you, so we recommend you store them according to their primary use: white distilled vinegar is great for cleaning and bottling; rice vinegar is perfect for creating delicious dishes, and apple cider vinegar has wonderful medicinal and cleaning properties. Store 4 gallons of vinegar for cleaning and 2 gallons of vinegar per person for cooking, preserving, and medicinal uses.

PRESERVING YOUR OWN

Now that you've learned how to store well, it is time to learn how to preserve well. Storing food for a family of 4 to last for months can be very expensive. One way to reduce your expenses is to grow your own food and preserve it. In fact, learning how to preserve your food is a lifelong skill that will serve you well, no matter your situation.

It is a great way to stop relying on archaic government-assisted food distribution systems and corporate supermarkets and learn to lean on yourself instead. We like to think that, although we can't trust many people or corporations in life, we can trust ourselves.

Therefore, the more skills you learn for survival, the more you can trust yourself no matter what situation you find yourself in. The skill of preserving your food is easy. You can preserve food by:

1. **Canning**

Almost any food can be canned, from fruits to vegetables to soups. To can your food, you will need to invest in a home canning kit. It will contain the following equipment:

- 1 pressure canner
- Quart or pint cans
- Can lids and bands (both wide mouth and regular)*
- Can lifter
- Canning rack (optional equipment to use when water bath canning)
- Can Funnel
- Canning salt

Note: Always use new lids. Never reuse lids when canning to avoid contamination.

The kit will cost you about $200. If you plan on canning just fruit, a water bath canner is good enough because the high acidity of the fruit will kill all bacteria.

To can your fresh produce at home, ensure the fruits are juicy and ripe and the vegetables are crisp. Wash them thoroughly, then cut off the blooms. Blanch the vegetables, killing all bacteria, and then can.

Ensure cooked food, such as meat, chili, and soup, is cooked thoroughly before canning.

2. Dehydrating

Moisture gives bacteria the ideal environment for growth. By dehydrating your food, you prevent bacteria from growing, causing your food to last a long time. Dehydration has been used for centuries, especially in hot countries where food spoils quickly. Today, thanks to electric dehydrators, dehydrating your food is very safe. You can dehydrate meat, fish, spices, fruit, and vegetables. Once dehydrated, food can last for years.

Even better, there are delicious recipes online for dehydrating your food. This way you don't have to have the same old dehydrated fruit or vegetables. You can mix it up to have a delicious variety of dehydrated food on hand for survival. These dehydrators typically cost between $60 and $250, depending on the quality you want.

Dehydrating food involves washing it and then drying it thoroughly. It is a skill that requires a fair bit of practice, especially since fresh foods need different methods of dehydration. We recommend cookbooks or video tutorials to help you get started.

3. Smoking

To smoke meat, you essentially dry it over wood chips to give it an additional layer of flavor. Using different types of wood chips will give you a distinct flavor to your meat. For example, beef jerky is made from smoked meat.

4. Root cellar

A root cellar is like nature's pantry. It keeps your food at a stable temperature, with the right amount of humidity to keep it fresh for long. You will need to make sure that you use wood shelving because wood shelving retains neither cold nor heat. It also allows for good air circulation, which food needs to stay fresh.

Likewise, food stored in root cellars needs to be kept with plenty of space in between to allow for air circulation. These fresh produce store well in root cellars:

- Carrots
- Onions
- Pumpkins
- Cabbage
- Potatoes
- Squash
- Pears
- Beets
- Turnips
- Apples
- Leeks
- Garlic
- Unripened tomatoes

To store your produce in a root cellar, harvest them without washing off the soil. The soil will keep the produce cool, preserving them. Lay them flat on the shelves and check that none of them are bruised. Bruised and rotten produce stored with healthy produce will rot the whole batch of produce with alarming speed. You can lose all your produce just from one bruised or rotten crop, so be very careful to check for these before storing them.

5. Curing

Curing uses the same processes as smoking and dehydration. When curing food, you take out all the moisture from the food using sea salt or kosher salt, preventing bacteria from growing as a result. After salting the meat, you have to hang it up to dry, ensuring that air can reach it from both sides to draw out all the moisture evenly.

6. Sugaring

Sugaring is like curing. A surface coated with crystal or granulated sugar is inhospitable to bacteria. To sugar a food, dry it completely first, then coat the surface in sugar. While sugared meats and vegetables may not taste nice, they are still foods that will ensure your survival. Sugared fruit is, of course, delicious.

7. Pickling

When you pickle food, you place it in antimicrobial conditions that are severely inhospitable for bacteria. This usually means placing it in brine or vinegar. You can pickle very many foods, including meats, eggs, vegetables, and even some fruits. Like sugaring, pickling food can change the texture and taste of the food. However, when in survival mode, you are more concerned with getting enough calories and nutrients than the taste or texture of your food. Luckily, your brain is so focused on achieving this goal in survival mode that you can wolf down food that you would turn your nose up at in everyday life.

8. Fermentation

Fermenting foods involves breaking down the carbohydrates in food and converting them into alcohol or acids to preserve them. Fermentation is the process we use to create cheese, beer, and yogurt. It is one of the oldest methods for preserving food in human history, so you will find plenty of tutorials and instructions on how to ferment your food.

GROWING YOUR OWN

To preserve your own food, you have to first grow your own food. Growing your own food is a skill that will benefit you in most situations in life. Unfortunately, most people today have become too complacent, comfortable, and lazy to grow their food. Thanks to their over-reliance on supermarkets and takeout restaurants, you will have noticed that people are becoming not only lazy but obese and unhealthy.

For people like you who want to stay healthy and live long, growing your food is a great way to avoid the poison and the complacency of modern living. It is a wonderful reversion to the traditional way of life that served our grandparents very well.

When you grow your own food, you eat a healthier, more nutritious diet. What's more, you are more active because you are always in your garden, working the land. Indeed, there are a lot of ways in which growing your own food benefits you as a prepper—ways that will be discussed in more depth in Chapter 11.

SURVIVAL TASK

Answer the following questions:

- How much food do you currently have stored?
- Do you have a rough food plan?
- How long will this last you?
- Do you feel that, if you were faced with a disaster scenario, you could feed yourself comfortably?

Check in with these questions, making sure you have a plan, or that you are, at least, thinking about making a plan. This is vital to be fully prepared for a variety of likely outcomes. One such outcome is a lack of power during a disaster. Without electricity, our traditional methods of preserving food become useless. So, alternative methods for preservation are really important. Likewise, without electricity, our traditional methods of cooking food also become useless, as will be examined in the next chapter.

Key Chapter Takeaway

- You can store all the food in the world, but if you come back to your food during a disaster to find that it has been contaminated, then all your hard work would have amounted to nothing.
- There are four types of contamination that come from not properly storing food: microbial, physical, allergenic, and chemical.
- Ideally, you want to store your food in a cool and dry basement storage room or pantry, placed on sturdy shelves that allow you to access and rotate your food regularly.
- Ideally, you also just want to start with what you have and slowly build on that.
- Ensure that your food is always stored on heavy-duty shelving to prevent spills and breakage and rotate your food regularly to avoid eating expired food.
- When storing food, store food that is very easy and practical to store and cook.

- Store calorie-dense foods that can last you a long time.
- Storing food for a family of 4 to last for months can be very expensive. One way to reduce your expenses is to grow your own food and preserve it.
- For people who want to stay healthy and live long, growing your own food is a great way to avoid the poison and the complacency and poison of modern living.

In the next chapter, you will learn how to cook your food with no electricity or power.

Chapter Five: Survival Cookery

In a disaster situation, conventional cooking techniques may be useless since they often rely on piped gas or electricity, which might not be available. Therefore, it is important to have other options.

This chapter will teach you how to cook food without power and how to create an outdoor oven to cook the food you stored. Now you know how to store enough food, you need to know how to cook it too. Although much of the food you store can be eaten cold, having a hot meal can do so much for your morale. Plus, you will still need to cook your carbs, grains, and legumes.

Survival cooking, at its heart, is creative cooking. You need to think of alternative ways to cook your food without an electric cooker, oven, or microwave on hand. Using the framework: O.U.T., you can keep in mind the different options available to you for cooking.

- ***O***ven cooking
- ***U***nconventional cooking.
- ***T***raditional cooking.

WAYS TO COOK FOOD WITHOUT POWER

One of the most bizarre parts of experiencing a disaster is the lack of energy. We are so used to energy that we take it for granted. But once it is gone, you realize just how much we rely on and depend on energy for survival. For one, many foods need to be cooked to become ingestible and digestible. Even if you eat them raw, your body cannot break them down small enough to extract the much-needed vitamins and minerals. For another, many perishable foods go bad surprisingly fast if not placed in the fridge or freezer.

Familiarizing yourself with ways to cook food without power is a much-needed survival skill that will keep you fed, healthy and happy during a disaster.

Some of the best ways of cooking food without power are the more traditional methods. These are methods we often use when camping, hiking, or simply going outdoors. They continue to be popular despite the advancements in electrical cooking methods because they are tried and tested methods of cooking a nice, hot, tasty meal when electricity is not practical. As well as the traditional methods of cooking outdoors, this chapter will include some more unconventional methods that you may never have heard of before, methods that will be incredibly useful when you are starving and need to eat.

Without power, you can cook using:

1. BBQ grill

A backyard barbeque grill or smoker is a handy way to cook your food. It is most likely that you have used one before or you have seen others use it before, so it doesn't take too long to master. Also, you can choose to use a dual propane/charcoal BBQ grill. With a dual grill, you can choose to use one source of fuel if you run out of the other. It is also helpful because you can pick up sticks and pieces of wood to burn for fuel should you run out of both charcoal and propane.

Another advantage is that you can cook side dishes or boil water using a barbecue grill that comes with a side burner.

As always, store plenty of charcoal (and wood), as well as tanks full of propane to last you months without power.

Barbecue grills can be quite big and heavy, especially if you need to cook for a large survival party. Consequently, you will need to consider where to store your barbecue grill.

2. Open fire

Most people have experience cooking on an open fire. Whether it's roasting chestnuts, marshmallows, roasting meat, or warming up a can of beans while camping, an open fire has always been an ever-present source of cooking for mankind. All you will need is clean burning wood and a fire-safe, non-toxic metal stands to place your cooking pans and kettles over the open fire. It takes a bit of practice to start one and to use one effectively, but a few tries are enough to give you the experience you need.

Be careful when using open fires to avoid the fire spreading and destroying the surrounding area.

3. Volcano stoves

A volcano stove is a small, portable stove, often used for camping purposes. They are collapsible and easy to store, taking up very little space, unlike BBQ grills. Even better, they are just as efficient whether fueled by propane, charcoal, or wood. They can be stored as an alternative to a barbecue grill in case of emergencies.

4. Solar ovens

Solar ovens are a great alternative to conventional cooking if you will be bugging in within your own home. The best advantage of a solar oven is that it requires no energy source since it is powered by the sun. Nonetheless, it is not a good primary source of cooking because you cannot cook during overcast days. You will also be limited to cooking between 11:00 am and 4:00 pm on sunny days.

Solar ovens trap the heat of the sun using a solar panel. This heat is transferred to the stove, which then cooks your food. A solar oven does not differ significantly from leaving your can of soup in the sun to heat. The only difference is you trap the heat to heat or cook your food faster in a solar oven.

Some solar ovens do not work well, so do your research before making a purchase. Sometimes, the paint inside solar ovens peels off. You should keep high-temperature barbecue black spray paint on hand to respray it when this happens.

5. Camp stoves

Propane camp stoves are a handy non-conventional cooking method. They need to be fueled by propane and must be used outdoors. Camp stoves are also usually small, so you won't be able to cook much food on it at the same time.

6. Fondue sets

Fondue sets are magnificent for heating food during a disaster—as long as you use an alcohol-burning one. It also means you will need to store some cooking alcohol on hand along with your other alternative sources of power.

Unconventional Cooking Techniques

There are a lot of ways for cooking and heating your food. You just need to be creative. Your primary goal when cooking or heating food is to get it hot. What we mean by this is that you need a source of heat. Once you find a source of heat, the rest is history.

Likewise, as a prepper, you must have an emergency plan for your emergencies. It may sound silly but, simply put, when you are in a disaster and you don't have your traditional cooking methods on hand, you need another emergency cooking method to cover your original disaster cooking plan. A good prepper always has a Plan B, should your Plan A not work out. A great prepper will also have a back-up Plan C, should Plan B fail.

Unconventional cooking methods are your Plan B for your traditional cooking methods.

Some good unconventional cooking methods for emergencies include:

1. Canned heat

Canned heat is also known as Sterno or gelled fuel. It is made from alcohol, which is then turned into a burnable jelly. You can purchase canned heat online from shopping retailers. You can also search camping stores and retailers that stock survival gear. Always keep a few supplies of canned heat in case of emergencies.

Be aware, however, that Canned Heat can be hard to contain just like an alcohol stove; and that the flame of canned heat can be hard to contain, just like an alcohol stove. They are also quite expensive to purchase, so you cannot stock too much of it. This is okay since you are only stocking a few supplies for emergencies only.

On the plus side, since they are made of alcohol jelly, canned heat doesn't evaporate and will, therefore, last, even when stored over a long period.

2. Tuna can and toilet paper stove

The tuna can and toilet paper stove is used by specialized armed forces internationally. Not only is it a great source of heat but it also makes a good emergency light.

Here is how to build one:

1. Open a small to medium can of tuna in oil, or any other can that has been used to store oil, like a can of sardines in oil.

2. Place 3 pieces of toilet paper flat over the tuna pieces so that they absorb the oil.

3. Once the toilet paper absorbs the oil, the toilet paper will create an airtight seal around the lid of the tuna can.

4. Light the toilet paper with a source of fire. The stove should burn for about 25 minutes–enough time to cook some food.

5. The fire will also cook the tuna underneath the toilet paper, which you can also then eat afterward.

3. Buddy burner

A buddy burner is quite similar to a tuna can stove except, this time, you empty the tuna can first.

Here is how to build one:

1. Cut out cardboard strips that are slightly thinner than the height of your tuna can. Ensure that you cut across the corrugated part. This way, the holes will be exposed on the sides.

2. Place them inside your empty tuna can.

3. Roll the strips of cardboard tightly, then fit them snugly inside the tuna can.

4. Melt either crayon or candle wax in a separate tin or pan, then pour onto the strips of cardboard. Never melt wax over a direct flame because it will easily catch fire.

5. Pour the melted wax over the cardboard strips. You can also use melted butter in place of melted wax.

6. Fill all the holes in the cardboard, and leave a bit of the cardboard roll exposed. This exposed cardboard will serve as the wick. Alternatively, stick a small piece of cardboard inside the can to use as a lighting wick. This will make it slightly easier to light your buddy burner.

7. Leave the wax to harden, then light your buddy burner. Once the wax hardens, you can light the buddy burner. You can stick a small piece of cardboard inside to serve as a wick and make lighting it easier if you wish.

4. Hay box oven

A hay box oven is as its name suggests. It is a box oven that traps heat. Once you heat your pot of food, for example, outside on an outdoor fire, you place it in the hay box oven. You then place hay all around the pot, close the box and leave it for 8-12 hours for the food to be cooked.

Hay box ovens work by trapping thermal heat and using this trapped heat to complete the cooking process. It is a great way to cook food that needs to be simmered over low heat for a long time, such as legumes and stews. Think of it as an emergency slow cooker. It works great if you can't stay outside for 12 hours, constantly checking up on your food, for example, if it is too cold or too hot outside. It is also great because you need very little fuel using a hay box oven since it relies on its own trapped heat.

Another significant benefit is that you can make your hay box oven should you need to do so. All you will need is an insulated box, for example, a cooler that you no longer use. You will then also need something insulated to place on top and beside your cooler to trap the thermal heat in, for instance, a cardboard box that you line with aluminum foil, as well as old, thick sweaters and blankets.

5. Tea light oven

Tea light ovens, also known as Home Emergency Radiant Cooking (HERC), work using tea lights. It works by using multiple tea lights at once to cook over a small pot. This is only an emergency use of tea lights because it will take up to 8 hours to cook a small pot of food. You will need to use an enclosed pot and place it atop of the tea lights. By doing so, the pot will trap heat and simmer the food.

As with the hay box oven, a tea light oven can be used for slow cooking over low heat. You can cook food like stews, soups, and mac and cheese over a tea light oven.

Remember that these techniques are more for emergency-based cooking. A more long-term method would be more appropriate (as discussed in the next part of this chapter). However, for emergencies, these would work well.

Creating a Wood-Fired Earth Oven

Whether you are bugging in your own home or bugging out elsewhere (as will be discussed in the next chapter), creating a wood-fired earth oven is a long-term solution for ensuring that you have a cooking method that does not rely on conventional cooking techniques.

Wood-fired ovens have been used for centuries by civilizations all over the world. Most societies have had a version of their wood-fired oven specifically because it works very well and is highly reliable. We see a wood-fired earth oven as a permanent replacement for an electric cooker or electric oven.

Even better, with a wood-fired earth oven, you do not have to rely on unconventional or traditional cooking methods unless in emergencies, or unless you only want to cook a little food and don't fancy lighting a whole fire in the oven.

If you live in a cold climate, a wood-fired earth oven is another way to keep warm when it is cold. Some societies traditionally built their ovens inside their homes as a source of heat and fire. We wouldn't recommend you build your oven indoors because modern homes have too many flammable materials.

Benefits of a Wood-Fired Oven

There are other great benefits of building your wood-fired oven. They include:

- You can bake a lot of delicious foods, including soft bread, crusty bread, and pizzas.
- It works like an electric oven. You can roast meats and fish, as well as baked dishes, such as savory and sweet pies and even cakes.
- It is very cheap to make since your key ingredient is the clay on the ground.

Build Your Own Wood-Fired Oven

Here is a detailed step-by-step guide for creating a wood-fired earth oven:

1. **The first steps for making your wood-fired earth oven**

Ensure you have enough mud to make the oven. The amount of clay you need depends on the size of the oven you want to build. While you can't gauge exactly how much clay you need, if you have enough clay covering the ground of your property, then this should be sufficient.

Get together all the tools you need, mainly a wheelbarrow, a shovel, a tape measure, some large buckets, scraps of wood, a plastic tarp, red bricks, and sculpting tools (kitchen utensils will work well for this).

Your next step is to prepare a base for the oven. You can prepare the base on the ground. Conversely, if you plan to use your oven frequently, then place your base at a waist-length level. You do not want to have to bend to the ground every time you need to put in or take out your food from the oven.

If you decide to place your oven base at waist-length, raise the base using miscellaneous objects, such as broken-up concrete, logs, or rocks.

2. Making the wood-fired oven floor

Your next step is to make the oven floor. A good measurement is between 20 and 27 inches. If you plan to bake things that are taller than 27 inches, then make the floor larger.

Lay red or fire bricks on prepared tamped sand that has been smoothed. The sand must be between 4 to 6 inches deep. You can also use used mortar-free bricks.

To set the bricks. set one brick leveled and solid. Next, hold the second brick level, just above the sand, gently setting its long side to the long side of the first brick. Continue this process, setting each brick down flat and firm without wiggling them. Tap down bricks so that they are all level with each other.

3. Making a form

Pile moist sand on the set bricks, then shape them to a few inches higher than half of the oven floor's width. For example, if your oven is 24 inches wide, the sand form should be 12 inches high.

Calculate the interior height by measuring the distance from the top to the floor. Multiply this height by 63% to determine the measurement for your oven door.

4. Mixing mud for your outdoor oven

You must use soil below the topsoil to build your oven. You can either mix one part clay with one to three parts sharp (builder's) sand or use it as it is. Note that pure clay subsoil usually shrinks and cracks more than a sand mix. You can find soil in your backyard, road cuts, construction sites, or river banks.

To verify that it is clay subsoil, check that it feels slippery, sticky, and a bit greasy (not crumbly and floury). Wet the soil by adding water a little at a time. Use your hands and feet to mix, but check for debris first. You can also just use your feet by stomping with boots on. Mix until it begins to clump like pie crust dough, or until you can roll the dough into snakelike ropes that bend easily. To test it, drop a ball from chest height. If it breaks, add a little water.

Make a test brick. Once dried, the brick would be hard and dense with little to no cracks.

5. Build your wood-fired oven

Lay sheets of wet newspaper flat on your sand form. This stops the mud walls from sticking to the sand form. Cover the sand form with a 3-4 inches thick layer of mud, maintaining an even thickness. You will cut out the doorway later, so don't worry about that.

Once the oven dome form is completed, pack the mud material using a flat board until it sits solidly against the form. It shouldn't stick to the board but, if it does, your mix is too damp and needs to dry for longer. Once you confirm the first layer is dried, add more layers. Last, add a fine finish plaster, if you so desire.

6. Remove the oven sand dome form

Your doorway needs to be 63 percent of the height of your oven. Its width should be 33-50 percent of the oven's inner diameter. Outline in the mud where you want the door to be, then slowly carve out the door, stopping once you hit the newspaper layer. But first, press gently on the outline with your fingers. If it leaves a dent, it is not dry enough to be dug out. Wait until it feels like leather, then try again. Be patient as this step can take days, and even weeks!

7. Make your outdoor oven beautiful

Polish the outside of your oven. You can draw patterns on the surface or build a mud extension, like a bench. You should also think about building a roof with sticks and mud.

No matter how you choose to decorate, do not cover the oven with cement or paint. It needs to breathe, otherwise, trapped moisture will render it useless.

8. Making the oven door

Finally, cut out the door. It doesn't need to be a perfect fit as wet cloth draped over it adds much-needed moisture to your food when baking. Your oven is now ready to use, barring one step.

Build your first fire and allow the smoke to come out. There will be no more black soot on the inside of the dome once the oven is dry (after two-three hours). Your oven is now ready to use.

By preparing this oven in advance, you will be ready to go off-grid, whether or not there is a catastrophe. There are other benefits, such as making great pizza nights! Even if you have never experienced a disaster or emergency, having a wood-fired oven still has many great uses. Since they last for many decades, if built well, you are guaranteed to use them for your entire life. In that case, they are a substantial investment no matter how you look at it.

SURVIVAL TASK

Try a few of the emergency cooking methods after finishing the chapter. This means you will know exactly what to do should the worst happen and you'll be prepared for the worst.

Key Chapter Takeaway

- Survival cooking is, at its heart, creative cooking.
- You need to think of alternative ways to cook your food without an electric cooker, oven, or microwave on hand or you will starve.
- Many foods need to be cooked to become ingestible and digestible. If you try to eat them raw, your body cannot extract the much-needed vitamins and minerals.

- Some of the best ways of cooking food without power are the more traditional, tried, and true methods. These are methods we often use when camping, hiking, or simply outdoors.

- The most important thing when cooking food without power is to find a source of heat.

- When you are in a disaster and you don't have your traditional cooking methods on hand, you need another emergency cooking method to cover your original disaster cooking plan.

- Most societies have a version of their wood-fired oven because it works very well and is highly reliable.

- A wood-fired earth oven is a permanent replacement for an electric cooker or electric oven.

- By preparing this oven in advance, you will be prepared for going off grid, whether or not there is a catastrophe.

In the next chapter, you will learn how to create shelters in case you need to evacuate your home.

Chapter Six: Creating Shelter

Although you will prefer to bug-in at home during an emergency, in situations where you would have to evacuate your home, it is essential to have other shelters or safe houses prepared. As we said in the previous chapter, a good prepper always has a Plan B to cover Plan A, should your Plan A not work out. A great prepper will also have a back-up Plan C, should Plan B fail.

The rule of 3 states that you need three things to survive: air, water, and food. These are your three foremost concerns after a disaster. Once you've taken care of these needs, you will want to focus on another basic necessity for survival: shelter.

Have you ever stopped to consider why humans of all civilizations and cultures have built some sort of shelter, even if it might just be a makeshift tent? Well, because sleeping outside in the rain for hours is not ideal.

Neither is sitting in the sun during a heat wave, being exposed not just to the elements, but to predators and venomous creatures and critters. Consequently, in the hierarchy of human survival, shelter comes after the rule of 3.

In fact, most times, shelter can be more important than water and food. Why? Well, you can die within the space of a few hours in unideal conditions. Essentially, it is impossible for you to go out looking for water if you cannot find shelter to protect yourself from a storm for a few hours.

Shelter protects you from long-term exposure to the elements and the outside world, which could cause hypothermia (becoming too cold), hyperthermia (becoming too hot), and many other dangerous conditions. Your body is always trying to thermoregulate itself. This means that it is always trying to keep you at a constant human temperature of 98.6°F (37°C) in order to keep you alive.

Shelter is simply your way of empowering your body to do its job of keeping you alive and well. The only thing that will kill you faster than a lack of shelter is a lack of air. We like to think of it this way: you can survive a day in a good, dry, warm shelter without water. However, you can be as hydrated and satiated as you want, but you will not survive a day out in the snow without shelter.

Humans have many more ways of keeping warm without shelter, such as coats, fur, and fire, but these are only temporary measures. You will need shelter after only a few days.

Ideally, a shelter should be able to not just keep you at the human temperature, but even warmer. It should keep you dry, repelling wind and rain, and be able to radiate heat off of human bodies to keep the entire shelter warm. Additionally, it should be able to conserve heat from other sources, like fire, and give you the ability to sleep off the ground, so that you do not lose your body heat. Last, it should be able to provide shade, but also keep you cool in hot temperatures.

When we talk about shelter, most people think of big comfortable tents or even cabins. The good news is you don't have to build a cabin unless you want to. Something as simple as a tent made of sticks and a reflective blanket, or a cave tunneled out of a snowbank, will meet all these conditions.

Thankfully today, we also have many more sophisticated ways of building makeshift shelters, whether long-term or short-term. This chapter will explore the options available to you, including bug-out shelters, bunkers, and other longer-term shelters. But, first, you must remember to be ***PIOUS*** when thinking of shelter. That means that:

- ***P***repare to bug in and out.
- ***I***n a disaster, everyone is an enemy.
- **O**n the move, build temporary shelters.
- ***U***nderground bunkers are Plan C.
- **S**helter before food and water.

Bugging In vs Bugging Out

Before we get into the different options available to you, however, you need to understand the key pros and cons of bugging out and bugging in. These are very common terms thrown around in the prepper community, so you might wonder how to choose which is the best option for you in different disaster scenarios. This table will help you figure out the benefits and downsides to both bugging in and bugging out.

	Bugging In	**Bugging Out**
PROS	If someone in your survival party is physically unable to travel long distances or has medical needs, bugging in is the clear winner.	When shit hits the fan, bugging out can keep you from deadly disease or violence, you can avoid becoming infected or hurt by going off-grid.

	Bugging in is much less stressful than bugging out. You don't have to carry heavy things, worry about leaving something essential behind, or about making shelter.	Preparing to bug-out removes the anxiety of a possible disaster. You are more flexible because you are ready to leave at any time.

	Houses are very reliable and keep us safe from the elements - very cold, winter conditions and very hot summer conditions.	You have more space when you bug-out for gardening, hunting, and other survival techniques.
	You get the familiarity of being around people who know you. Your neighbor is much more likely to look out for you and share	You have to learn a lot of skills to be able to bug out. While it is a lot of work, these skills will never leave you.

	with you, and vice versa. By building a survival community, you are more likely to survive.	
	You have a well-stocked survival pantry, meaning you don't have to forage or hunt for food. You also have more places to hide your food, in case of break-ins.	You don't have to worry about being hit by either natural or artificial disasters. You can choose to bug-out in a location that is free of both human interference and a history

		of natural disasters.
CONS	You could be caught in civil unrest, riots, and other deadly, violent eruptions in urban and suburban areas.	Bugging out is stressful for the elderly, sick, children, and pets, so use it only as a final option if you have any of these in your survival party.
	In an area that regularly has natural disasters, bugging in can have severe risks.	You are only able to carry limited medical supplies. Any disease, accident, or

	It may be the least safe choice.	illness could be hard to treat, even an emergency phone call might be too late by the time emergency services get to you.
	Your neighbors, even if they know you very well, can turn against you. Remember that disaster brings out the worst in humans. If you have supplies, you	You can only carry enough food for a few days before you need to start looking for your food, either by hunting or foraging.

	have to be prepared to defend yourself.	
	The COVID-19 pandemic showed us that governments can–and will–keep citizens from leaving their homes or even moving freely. If you decide to bug in, you could become trapped, with no supplies, and when disaster worsens.	Bugging out requires a lot of physical exertion. You will get very tired and depleted of essential nutrients and electrolytes. You need to be physically fit to survive bugging out.

	Bugging in will mean that you have limited space. Your family may start to feel suffocated the longer you have to stay in this one space to survive.	You will need to defend yourself against possible predators, harmful animals, looters, or any other person who may want to harm you.

Based on the pros and cons in the table above, it might be tempting to think that one method is better than another. You will want to choose either bugging out or bugging in because one method will suit your specific situation better.

Nevertheless, we would advise you not to be tempted to think that just one option will work for you. Remember, always have a Plan A, a Plan B, and a Plan C. In this case, you can only have two plans, so choose both.

This means that you choose one primary method of survival, but also prepare for the second method as a backup option. The method you choose will be whichever one applies best to you, has less risk, and has a higher chance of survival, based on the pros and cons. So, while you may prepare your house with two years' worth of food supply for bugging in, you will also need to learn how to defend yourself as a contingency plan, should you need to leave your home and bug out.

Ways To Fortify Your Home To Bug In

As you've seen from the table above, one con of bugging-in is that you may have to deal with looters or even violent rioters. In a disaster, everyone is an enemy. What this really means is that anyone can turn on you once the desperation for food, water, air, shelter, or medicine gets to them. So, the best way to defend yourself is to fortify your home. This reduces your need to use force and violence.

To fortify your home for bugging in:

1. **Never spill the beans.**

A good prepper is secretive. That means you never tell people you are a prepper.

Other than the people in your survival party, nobody else must know that you keep drinkable water and a year's food supply because once shit hits the fan, they will come knocking. If you refuse to help them, things will quickly turn violent against you and your survival party.

There are other ways for people to find out that you are a prepper without you speaking about it. For example, they could find receipts from your purchases, or they could smell your cooking or see you drinking a glass of juice when the juice has not been sold in supermarkets for months.

Hence, you need to camouflage yourself so that, from the outside, you look to be living the same life like everyone else around you during a disaster. Tear up receipts after purchase. Dress the same and act the same. Cover your windows and lock all windows and doors when cooking. You may even think about complaining to your neighbors about not having enough to eat. Yes, it is manipulative, but once the shit hits the fan, the societal rules change and it is a survival of the fittest situation. It is better to be manipulative than end up dead because a hungry neighbor looted your home for food.

2. Defend your perimeter.

The best offense is a good defense, so guard your perimeter. It is best to simply keep people from entering your home in the first place. However, you need to be inconspicuous about it. If you suddenly put up a tall fence, your neighbors will realize that you have something to protect. Defend your perimeter by putting barbed wire and broken glass on the fence and on the surrounding perimeter near the fence.

Plant defensive plants that are very thorny and have loads of prickles, like the century plant, firethorn, tomato porcupine, bougainvillea, and Spanish bayonet. They are nature's barbed wire.

You can also use trees and shrubs to stop others from looking into your home. However, do so strategically, so that you also can see if anyone else is looking into your home, trying to snoop and find ways of breaking in.

Ensure that there is open space between the fence and your actual home so that you can see whoever is outside trying to get in. Don't be afraid to use warning signs, such as "trespassers will be shot." Although, if you do have a dog on the premises, do not use a warning sign advertising this as your pet could be stolen for food.

Last, good old-fashioned hidden cameras and motion lights work superbly well. Use a solar-charged one in case of power outages.

3. **Fortify your home.**

The next step of protection from anyone who makes it past your perimeter is the outer area of your home, including your walls, doors, and windows. Use heavy, solid wood or metal-insulated doors and install them with longer set screws and strike plates. Add high-quality, single-cylinder deadbolt locks and door jammers.

Door jammers could save your life by buying you some time to escape. Secure your window sills with defensive plants and install burglar bars over your windows. Install window locks and add security film to your window panes to strengthen them against breakage. Last, you can set up sandbags to defend yourself against any armed intruders using a gun.

You also have the option of setting booby traps, such as trip wires, perimeter alarms, corn flour explosives, and pit traps. Still, we don't recommend this option. They may look cool in movies, but they are deadly and can land you in legal trouble.

4. **Build a safe room.**

Your last option for protection in a bug-in scenario is a safe room/bunker. Stockpile your safe room or bunker with enough food and supplies to keep you alive for months. Remember to be inconspicuous. This means that your safe room does not look like any other room out of the ordinary. That way, you do not alert intruders to the purpose of this room or to the fact that you're in there.

Make sure you have enough sleeping space and moving room for every member of the survival party. You will also need to make sure it is in a location in your home where everyone in your survival party can reach quickly in case of danger or intruders.

It is difficult to find space for a safe house if your house is small. Here, you'll need to be creative to find a space that will work for you.

Bug-out Shelters

Here are some bug-out shelters that are available to you, whether you live in an urban or rural area. Be aware that these are temporary shelters that you can use for only a few weeks before you will need to find more permanent shelter. Many of these temporary shelters can be used while you are on the move to safety. Either way, they can help you wait out the disaster and its aftermath until you can safely return home.

1. Urban Bug-out Shelters

Underneath Staircases

Assuming your staircase is small, it can provide a cozy nook for waiting out a disaster, staying safe, and also hiding in case you need to.

It can be a good option, as it is structured similar to a lean-to and one can tuck in behind and be fairly invisible. You will feel cramped/claustrophobic if you have to stay there for more than a few weeks.

Shipping Containers

Shipping containers are ready-made, sturdy, totally weatherproof, and you can find them all over the place. They will block out wind and water—if they are in good shape—and keep you safe from dangerous animals.

If you choose one that looks dilapidated on the outside and is in a remote area, you will also be safe from other people. If someone stumbles across one, they might wander in, looking for shelter and/or supplies too. You will also need to be very careful not to accidentally lock yourself in.

Dumpster Shelters

The first thing you think of when you hear dumpsters is the horrible smell. Yet, dumpsters are a great temporary shelter if you can withstand the smell or find one that doesn't smell too bad. As with shipping containers, dumpsters attract both people and animals looking for food, shelter, and other supplies. They do protect you from the rain and wind and they are found almost everywhere.

To prevent unwanted visitors, wrap cordage around the lid, then tie it around your waist.

2. Rural Bug-out Shelters

Lean-To Shelters

A lean-to is the easiest temporary shelter to construct. You only need some building scraps and a couple of large pieces of cardboard to build one.

You can also search for insulating materials, like styrofoam, to keep you off the ground so you can stay warm and dry. Alternatively, you can use wooden pallets to stay off the ground.

As with most temporary shelters, one of your main concerns is staying hidden. People searching for supplies will target your lean-to. Hide your shelter behind debris or any leftover scrap once you complete your lean-to.

Debris Hut

We like to think of debris huts as nature's sleeping bags. They naturally trap your body heat so that you can keep warm through the night. You can also build them with enough room to move around a bit so that you are not cramped.

To build your own debris hut, create a bipod with two poles, measuring four feet in length. Lay a ridge pole, measuring eight feet, against it. Lean branches on both sides, ensuring it is at a 45-degree angle. Lastly, pile several feet of debris at the top to create a thick layer of insulation.

The good thing about debris huts is that they are naturally hidden thanks to all the debris you pile on them, so most people would not even notice it. Try not to sleep on the ground. Instead, use wood pallets or insulating materials, like styrofoam.

Emergency Blanket Shelter

Emergency blankets are big enough to build a temporary shelter in most situations. Thanks to their reflective surface, however, they are very shiny, which means they will attract nearby animals and people.

You can set up an emergency blanket like you would a tarp, using any nearby sticks to keep it upright. You can also tie it to a tree or peg it down into the ground.

Creating a Bunker

Our mantra is that a prepper always has a Plan A and a Plan B. A good prepper also has a Plan C. Bugging in and bugging out are your Plans A and B. whichever one fits your needs will obviously be your chosen Plan A. But you should know that there is a Plan C in this case: an underground bunker. A Plan C is always nice for your peace of mind, and if you decide to go down this route, it will become Plan A. But it is still optional and if, after reading this chapter, you decide that a bunker is too expensive, or it takes too much effort, then you can skip this step in your prepping plan.

Gone are the days when people built bunkers because they were terrified of a Nuclear War. Now we are terrified of even more things that could happen, such as:

1. **Natural disasters**

Tornadoes

Scarily enough, natural disasters are becoming more constant. In the event of something like a tornado, you may not be able to get to your bug-out location on time.

Heatwave

Underground bunkers are also really cool and will keep you comfortable during a heatwave.

Floods and Fires

Be careful not to use an underground bunker in case of fires or floods, unless your bunker is specifically designed to handle these natural disasters.

2. Artificial Disasters

As society becomes more and more unfair, we will see more artificial disasters. To be honest, this is very scary, but don't forget that therefore you became a prepper in the first place: to banish fear by being prepared.

Nuclear War

As more countries join the nuclear arms race, some using their “bomb” as a threat to adjoining countries or even the superpowers, the possibility of a nuclear war is as real as it was in the 1980s.

During the 80s, nuclear fallout shelters for private use became quite popular, albeit controversial. Some of these shelters were factory-built, fitted out, and shipped to the site where they were buried deep in the ground and surrounded by concrete. Others were made on-site using reinforced concrete and then fitted out before covering in dirt.

Both of these options are still available today, but they are extremely expensive and the technical requirements are quite stringent to withstand a nuclear blast and radiation fallout. They require emergency power, air filtration systems, and air-tight doors. Not something that can be constructed by the keen amateur.

EMPs

Bunkers are also built to withstand electromagnetic pulses (EMPs). EMPs occur after a nuclear explosion happens, statically charging the lower atmosphere. EMPs will damage all your electronic devices, as well as electrical power grids, leaving you with no ability to contact loved ones or emergency services.

Similarly, a bunker will protect you from Coronal Mass Ejections (CMEs). These are released plasma and magnetic fields ejected from our sun. Once CMEs reach Earth, they can do damage to electrical power grids.

Long-Term Power Outages

With CMEs or EMPs, you could suddenly find yourself without electricity for weeks and even months. Our entire survival system depends on electricity and energy. Most supermarkets only stock food that lasts one or two days at most. Food will go bad and farms will start being looted as chaos ensues. As humans turn on each other, your best bet for survival is a bunker.

Pandemic

Pandemics can be natural or artificial, but, without a doubt, they are always a danger to you. We saw with the recent COVID-19 pandemic outbreak how easy it is for pathogens to spread and infect the entire Earth's population. It took just a few weeks, but with an even more powerful superbug, it can take just days. We also saw with COVID-19 how isolation helped stop the spread of superbugs. If a bunker isn't a great place to isolate, then we don't know what is.

Cyber Attack

Our entire lives are governed by the internet and our electronic devices. With widespread cyber attacks, society would crumble within the space of days, leading to social breakdown.

Social Breakdown

We have seen more and more civil unrest in recent years, as society seems to break down, albeit slowly. It takes just one civil unrest to turn into an entire societal breakdown. In fact, it takes just one event to lead to an entire social breakdown, as we saw in the lead-up to World War I.

You never know what will lead to social breakdowns, so it is best to just be prepared by having a bunker.

How to Build a Bunker

Before you start digging, there are a few things you must consider. First, what is it you want to protect yourself from? As we mentioned earlier, nuclear bunkers are not something you can build yourself, so let's come down a level and look at the other natural and artificial disasters that you can defend against at a reasonable cost.

1. Choose Your Location

Your location must be in a safe, secret, and private area that is within walking distance of your house. As already discussed, bunkers do not fare well when introduced to fire or water, so avoid areas near bodies of water or flammable material, like dry grass.

Don't locate your bunker close to trees or vegetation because the roots will make it difficult to dig and you don't want to cut through them, as this could make trees unstable and kill off smaller plants.

2. Develop a Blueprint

Your bunker is designed for safety, security, and comfort—not luxury. This means that you're not wasting any space on unnecessary things, but you still need space to move around comfortably.

The best way to do this is to make the best use of vertical space. Go for bunk beds rather than a king-size bed. Install wall-mounted furniture, like tables and storage units. An open-plan design allows you to combine space for sitting, eating, and preparing food. You may have separate rooms for sleeping, which can be formed using timber and plasterboard partitions, but you certainly will need to separate the toilet area.

We recommend you plan for between 5-10 square feet of space per person. This will give you some idea of the area you need for your bunker. A long, narrow design is better than a square design, as this will keep the span of the roof to a minimum.

Consider also how you will get in and out of the bunker—steps or a ladder. Ladders are not suitable for a disabled person but they take up less room.

Draw your blueprint to scale, showing the correct wall thicknesses and where all the furniture and equipment will go. There are many free software packages available that you can use if you're no good at drawing.

3. Pick the Right Bunker Material

Your bunker must support the weight of the surrounding earth and the backfill material on top. There are several materials you can use, these are the most popular:

Metal Sheeting

Profiled or corrugated metal sheeting is water-resistant and sturdy, but it must be supported on a steel frame. The roof steelwork will need vertical support as well, which might impact your floor layout.

Metal sheeting will also need insulating and lining if you don't want to see the bare metal.

Concrete

Concrete is the best material for the floor slab, where it must be laid on a sheet of thick polythene (300 microns) to prevent water rising from the ground.

Concrete can also be used for the walls and roof, but it must be reinforced with steel bars or mesh, and again, protected from water ingress.

Wooden shuttering is required to form the walls and roof, which may even be left in place on the inside to make it easier to fix things.

Bricks and Blocks

Bricks and blocks are easy to lay and cheap to source. Blocks are quicker to lay being larger than bricks, but they're not as aesthetic.

For perimeter walls, it is best to build the outer leaf using dense concrete blocks and an inner leaf of brick with a cavity between them to prevent groundwater from penetrating the inside surface.

4. Get Your Permit

Don't start any construction work until you have a permit from your local building department or zoning board. For this, you will need your blueprint and a map of where your bunker will be located.

Depending on where you live, you may also need one or more of the following: grading permit, discretionary permit, plumbing permit, and electrical permit. If you intend to have ventilation equipment installed, you will also need a permit for that.

Armed with your permits, there is one more thing you must do before you start digging, and that is to call 811. This is the utility hotline and they will tell you where the pipes and lines are in the area where you want to dig.

5. Choose the Right Excavating Equipment

You're going to need an excavator (or mini-excavator) for this. Digging by hand is not only arduous and slow, but it is also dangerous at this kind of depth.

Set out the area of your bunker with pegs and rope using the dimensions on your blueprint. It's best to add a foot all around to allow for discrepancies in the digging.

6. Start Digging

The excavation needs to be as deep as your bunker plus around 2-3 feet for dirt cover.

Excavating is a hazardous operation and there are lots that can go wrong that can lead to injuries or even death. As a precaution, you must:

- Keep excavators and heavy equipment away from the edge of the excavation.
- Keep a ladder in the excavation at all times.
- Don't allow exhaust fumes from plant such as generators or vehicles to discharge over the excavation.
- Barrier around the excavation at the end of a day's work.

The type of soil you're digging into will inform you about the type of support you need. Cohesive soil has a high clay content, so the sides of the excavation should stay vertical while you build the walls. Granular soil contains sand and gravel, so you will have to support the sides or slope/bench them.

Sloping is done by cutting the trench wall at an angle, whereas benching is done by creating long benches that rise up the wall in steps.

7. Construct the Shelter

Start with the floor. We recommend using reinforced concrete for the floor because it is strong and forms a good base for the walls.

Once the base of your excavation is flat and free of vegetation, place a 4-inch layer of stone over the whole area and compact it. This will help drain away any groundwater and take up any ground movement. Place a 2-inch layer of sand over this so the surface is flat and free of any sharp stone.

Next, place a layer of polythene over the sand with about a foot left over at the edges, which should be turned up against the sides of the excavation.

It is quicker and cheaper to use a welded mesh reinforcement on the floor. This must be spaced 2 inches off the polythene so the concrete can get underneath it when it's poured.

If you're mixing your own concrete, a mix of 1 part cement, 2 parts sand, and 3 parts stone by volume will be strong enough.

With your base laid, you can build the shelter using the materials of your choice. You can even place a pre-fabricated shelter on the slab, or if your budget is tight, a shipping container, but this would have to be reinforced to withstand the pressure of the surrounding earth.

Remember, the walls need to be thick enough to support the roof, and the roof needs to be strong enough to support the dirt backfill. This may mean you have to incorporate steel beams and columns.

If you live in an earthquake zone, you may also need to reinforce your bunker with cross braces, movement-resisting frames, and shear walls. An engineer will advise you on this and any other structural issues you may have.

8. Acquire Key Living Equipment

Key living equipment will keep you alive while you are underground. You will need:

Ventilation/Air Filters

To provide fresh air and filter out air contaminants.

Water Filters

You will need a UV filter while living underground to destroy viruses and bacteria.

Waste Removal System

You need a way to get rid of toxic waste once you are off-grid in your bunker. This includes:

- A "poop tube" made with a PVC pipe. These are OK for short-term use and easy to set up.

- A composting toilet that converts waste into fertilizer that can be used for your plants. Composting toilets can get smelly in the enclosed space of your bunker.

- A wastewater pump and lift system. This system pumps your waste from the toilet to the ground level, keeping your bunker free of waste. Hand pumps avoid the need for an electrical supply.

A Backup Generator

Although you may have connected your bunker to your domestic electricity supply, there is no guarantee that this will be available after a catastrophic event. A backup generator will provide you with electricity for lighting and ventilation for as long as you have enough fuel.

Locate the generator somewhere outside your bunker or in its own below-ground storage unit because the exhaust fumes are highly toxic.

9. Stock Up On Provisions

Stock up on food and water provisions. See Chapter Four to decide what food and drinks to store. Some preppers argue that two weeks' worth of food is enough, but this is not a good idea.

In the event of a nuclear explosion or a biological/chemical attack, you may have to sit out the aftermath for up to six months before radiation or contamination levels subside enough for you to venture out. Therefore, six months should be considered the optimum period for storage purposes.

SURVIVAL TASK

Although bunkers can be more costly than other shelters, it could be life-saving, particularly if there was a nuclear attack. Seriously consider implementing a Plan C shelter option.

Take two minutes to think about a location where you could build a bunker. Look back over this chapter and come up with a few ideas on how you could structure your bunker. If a disaster is looming, then you need to be prepared!

Key Chapter Takeaway

- In case of situations where you would have to evacuate your home, it is essential to have other shelters or safe houses prepared.
- Shelter is even more important than water and food if you want to survive in the short and long term.

- Shelter protects you from long-term exposure to the elements and the outside world, which could cause hypothermia (becoming too cold), hyperthermia (becoming too hot), and many other dangerous conditions.

- Any shelter you build should keep you dry, repelling wind and rain.

- Don't be tempted to choose either bugging out or bugging in over the other just because one method suits your specific situations better. Prepare for both!

- If bugging in, you will need to fortify your home to protect you from looters or even violent rioters.

- On your way to your bug-out shelter, you will need to construct a temporary shelter to keep you alive. Your temporary shelter must protect you from wild animals, other humans, and the elements.

- An underground bunker is optional, but highly recommended, in case of natural/manmade disaster, or in case you cannot reach your bug-out location before disaster strikes.

In the next chapter, you will learn basic first aid techniques that you could use effectively on yourself and your family should anyone become injured.

CHAPTER SEVEN: FIRST AID

First aid is paramount to your survival during a disaster. As a prepper, you probably already know the importance of basic first aid. Yet, you might feel that you're too busy or it's not that important. Let's face it, all of us fall for that human arrogance of thinking that bad things will never happen to us: accidents only happen to other people.

Once the shit hits the fan, however, you can count on one thing: accidents will become more common. Even worse, it might be the case that emergency services are no longer functional. So, how do you and your survival party stay healthy and alive in that case? Plus, first aid is a lot more than staying alive. As a prepper, your first goal is staying alive, but you also have other goals. First aid will help you to:

1. **Reduce Danger**

Imagine that you are on your way to your bug-out location when a member of your survival party is bitten by an animal. They are bleeding profusely and will die within a few hours if you cannot bandage up the wound temporarily.

Also, you cannot continue your journey because you will leave a trail of blood that leaves you all in danger of both predators and other people who may want to rob you of your supplies - or worse! With first aid, you and your survival party can continue on your journey as quickly as possible without being exposed to predators, bad weather, and other humans.

2. Stay Healthy and Safe

Knowing how to take care of your basic medical needs keeps you healthy and safe from things like infections and medical complications. With first aid training comes great physical health, mental clarity, and a good immune system, all of which help you to stay healthy and alive during a disaster.

3. Prevent Your Conditions From Getting Worse

Leaving infections, wounds, and other health problems without treatment is just a gateway for your condition to get worse. This can lead to permanent disability or even death.

4. Be Confident

A great prepper is confident in their ability to survive. If not, you wouldn't prepare in the first place. You have taken the hard route of embracing the truth for what it is, so don't do things halfway. Now that you have embraced the truth, you want to have all the training you need, so that you can be confident that you will survive any scenario.

5. Increase Comfort

Nobody wants to be in pain - especially not during a disaster. A first aid kit, and first aid training, will reduce your survival party's chances of dealing with pain and suffering.

This chapter aims to inform you of basic first aid techniques that you could use effectively on yourself, your family, and anyone in your survival party, should anyone become injured. You will learn the importance of packing your own first aid kit, how many first aid kits you need, and the seven areas of first aid you need to prep for. Finally, you will understand why every good prepper has a ***PERM***:

- ***P***lace a first aid kit in every bag and location.
- ***E****nroll* in first aid class.
- ***R***egularly practice emergency scenarios.
- ***M***odify your first aid kit to fit your individual needs.

WHY YOU SHOULD PACK YOUR OWN KIT

Most preppers don't realize that they need to pack their own first aid kit. You can buy pre-packed first aid kits, which is highly convenient. The only problem is that they are created for everyday life. You use the tools in a first aid kit until you can either call emergency services or get to the hospital. At most, this will take you a day. This differs greatly from a first aid kit for when shit hits the fan. You don't know how long it's going to be until you can get to an emergency center or a hospital, so you must pack a heavy-duty trauma kit if you are to survive. With a heavy-duty trauma kit, you can take care of many different injuries, including serious traumatic injuries.

Seven Areas of First Aid For Preppers

These are the seven areas that you must pack in your first aid kit. Pack them in an easy-to-transport bag, so that you can grab the bag in case of emergencies.

1. Diarrhea

Diarrhea (watery bowel movements) can be caused by bacteria, viruses, parasites, medications, lactose intolerance, fructose intolerance, and any other digestive disorders. If left untreated, for even a few days, diarrhea can kill!

Remember that you will have to drink filtered water and possibly eat meat that you have to hunt yourself, without modern-day sanitation practices. To put it another way, diarrhea is an ever-present threat in disaster mode. Luckily, with the proper medication, you can prevent diarrhea by stocking the following:

- Activated charcoal tablets (to prevent poisoning).
- Enzyme supplement (for keeping your digestive system healthy).
- Fresh Green Black Walnut Wormwood Complex (for treating parasites).
- Heartburn relief, such as Tums or generic brands.
- Anti-diarrheal, for example, Imodium or any generic brand.
- Apple cider vinegar (to calm your stomach and indigestion and to prevent yeast infections).
- Electrolyte replenishing drinks, such as clear broth, Pedialyte (for children in your survival party), or just a teaspoon of salt mixed in apple juice.

2. Wound Treatment

Your first aid kit should be able to treat and protect against scrapes, punctures, cuts, burns, wounds, blisters, stings, bites too hot or too cold skin, and radiation burns. Care for your skin by stocking:

- Sunscreen lotions
- Soap
- Rubbing alcohol
- Neosporin/Polysporin
- Hydrogen Peroxide
- Moleskin
- Hydrocortisone anti-itch cream (for skin irritation)
- Bandages
- Burn Jel
- Blister Medic (for your feet)
- Ibuprofen (for relieving pain and swelling)
- Instant cold packs (for relieving pain and swelling)

- QuickClot
- Tweezers
- Sterile Scissors
- Splints
- Steri Strips skin closure

3. Upper Respiratory Infections

Don't let the medical-sounding name fool you. Upper respiratory infections just mean things like a cough, sore throat, and runny nose. It could also just mean things like lethargy or difficulty breathing. You will need:

- Antihistamine
- Halls Cough Drops
- Flash Light (for checking your throat in the dark)
- Thieves Oil (to prevent upper respiratory infections)

- Hydrogen Peroxide (to remove phlegm, mucus, or other secretions associated with a sore mouth)

4. Pain and Fever

Pain and fever can be caused by bacterial infections, heat, viruses, sunburn, and being exhausted, so pack:

- Mercury-free Analog Oral Thermometer
- Ibuprofen (for relieving pain, fever, and swelling)
- Chemical heat and cold packs
- Fish Mox (amoxicillin you can get over the counter without prescription)

5. Flu and Pandemic

Avoid the spread of flu, colds, bird flu, and swine flu by packing:

- Respirators (pandemic gloves)

- Nitrile Exam Gloves (stored in zip-lock bags to prevent contamination with nasty bugs)

- Pandemic Flu Kit. (Designed by Sundstrom, the Pandemic Flu Kit comes with a 99.997% absorption particle filter to filter out harmful particles like bacteria and viruses

- Infection Protection Kit (which contains eye protection, disposable thermometers, N95 respirator masks, vinyl gloves, and biohazard bags)

6. Dental Emergencies

For dental emergencies, carry:

- Hydrogen peroxide (for keeping your teeth clean)

- Hurricane Topical Anesthetic Gel

- Dental Medic. A dental first aid kit, Dental Medic, has the tools you need to treat dental pain and injury. It can serve as a replacement dental visit until you cannot get to a dentist

7. Personal Emergencies

For any other personal medical emergencies, stock:

- First aid for allergies/anaphylactic shock (Get two Epi-pens and Benadryl)
- First aid for diabetes (Store insulin in refrigerated containers and glucose tablets)
- First aid for eye care (Stock a few bottles of Visine. Make sure that the tip of the bottle does not hit another surface, or it will become infected)

This list is just a basic guide. What we recommend is that you take stock and think about what every member in your survival party truly needs. Then, you can tailor the kits to these needs.

8. What You Need To Do Now

Here is a step-by-step list of what you will need to do next to prepare.

1. Enroll in a First Aid Class. You can search for local first aid classes online to learn how to administer good first aid.

2. Practice emergency scenarios regularly. Practice emergency scenarios regularly. That way, it becomes routine for you. When an emergency occurs, sometimes it triggers our brain into freeze mode and we become paralyzed with shock. Practise beforehand to avoid being frozen in an actual emergency.

3. Evaluate your own requirements for an emergency first aid survival kit. What do you need specifically based on your needs and the needs of others in your survival party?

4. Buy a good first aid manual. Purchase two physical copies: one for home and one placed in your safety first aid kit. If you prepare more than two first aid kits,

then you need a first aid manual in all of them.

You can also download a PDF first aid manual to your smartphone to use for reference in case of emergencies. It is better to download it now when you have internet service. If you wait, there might not be 4G or Wi-Fi services available when you really need them.

9. **How Many First Aid Kits Do I Need?**

From this chapter alone, you now realize that you need multiple first aid kits for multiple purposes and to suit the different needs of everyone in your survival party.

You will also need a first aid kit in your bug-out bag, your get-home bag, your bug-in location, and your safe location. That is a lot of first aid kits to prepare, so evaluate what you will need in each kit. You may not need a dental first aid kit in your bug-out bag, for example, if you are using it to simply head to your safe location, where you have one.

Key Chapter Takeaway

- First aid is paramount to your survival during a disaster. It helps you stay safe from danger, stay healthy and comfortable, and prevents your health conditions from getting any worse.
- You need to pack your own heavy-duty trauma kit if you are to survive when SHTF.
- Your first aid kit must be tailored to meet your specific needs.
- Pack your first aid kit in an easy-to-transport bag, so that you can grab the bag in case of emergencies.
- It is important to enroll in a first aid class and practice emergency scenarios regularly.
- Buy good first aid manuals and keep one in every location and every bag.
- Download a PDF first aid manual to keep on your phone in case of emergencies.

In the next chapter, you will learn the different ways to create an off-grid waste system so that you can become more self-reliant and more likely to survive a scenario where you are forced to cope on your own.

Chapter Eight: Creating An Off-Grid Waste System

As we've seen throughout this book, once the shit hits the fan, all the normal utilities that we depend on so heavily as part of our everyday lives may become a thing of the past. By now, you should understand that, although disaster takes away the feelings of safety and security we take for granted in our everyday lives, prepping gives you the confidence and peace to accept a new reality.

This chapter deals with a utility that we take for granted: waste management. Why do we take it for granted? Well, we've become accustomed to a world where waste is disposed of regularly, or kept out of sight.

But all you need to do is spend a few days in a bunker with no waste management before you realize, with panic, how and why waste management is so important for staying healthy and alive. Apart from the horrendous, you will feel sick and may quickly fall ill - not to mention all the bugs and critters that will suddenly find their way to your bunker, home, or temporary shelter.

In this chapter, we will teach you how to avoid this nightmare by building your own waste management system, specifically greywater treatment systems and blackwater treatment systems. We will also show you how to get an off-grid water supply without a well.

What's more, with the information in this chapter, you can become more self-reliant and more likely to survive a scenario where you are forced to cope on your own, without usual waste management services available, whether it be government-assisted waste management, plumbers, or others. To meet your off-grid waste and water needs, you need to follow the three Rs:

- Reuse water
- Recycle your water and waste
- Rainwater is free to collect

GREYWATER TREATMENT

Before we move on to discussing the differences between greywater and blackwater, you need to know how cities and municipalities deal with their waste. Sewage systems have a simple mechanism where interconnected pipes collect all our waste into a treatment plant. There, the waste-filled water is filtered, disinfected, and treated until it is safe to use once more.

Greywater is separated from blackwater because it contains less waste, such as dirt, food waste, human skin cells, and cleaning products. With less toxic waste, like food waste and human waste, it contains less harmful pathogens and bacteria. That means you only need minimal treatment before you can reuse it in your garden and even toilet bowls. You can connect the pipes from your washing machines, sinks, tubs, and showers to collect gray water. Once you collect greywater, you can:

1. Leach It

To leach greywater, you connect your pipes to the irrigation system in your garden. That way you can use the greywater to water your plants. The soil helps break down and treat the water before the plants, then use it. You just have to ensure that your irrigation system only waters the soil, but doesn't touch your plants.

2. Treat It

You can purchase your own professional greywater system, to treat and disinfect your greywater. This usually comes in the shape of a compact closed bucket that passes the water through many stages of filtration. Then the filtered greywater moves into your irrigation system to automatically water your garden.

3. Refill Your Toilet

Last, you can replace the top of your toilet with a special sink and tap that connects to your toilet, allowing you to wash your hands with clean water. The sink then collects that greywater so that you can use it to flush your toilet.

Blackwater Treatment

Blackwater waste, as we've mentioned, has much more pathogens and bacteria in it because it contains more waste, especially harmful waste, including urine and feces. As a result, you will have to thoroughly treat it in your off-grid system before it can be reused. Another problem with blackwater waste is that it smells terrible.

If you cannot stand bad smells, then you might think of using blackwater waste as a Plan B to greywater waste. Or, you can leave the treatment systems outside far away from your home so that you do not smell it. There are three off-grid systems available to you. They are:

1. Composting Toilets

Composting toilets collect your human waste, then mix it with natural substances, such as pine needles, coffee grounds, and wood shavings. You then leave it in a bucket or container and give it time to turn into compost. To speed up the process, you can also add it to a composter, which provides enough heat to turn it completely into compost safe enough for your garden. A lot of preppers like to use Nature's Head brand of composting toilets.

You can also create your own DIY composting toilet. This is one drawback of being a prepper. Once the government and businesses stop functioning to meet your needs, you really do have to do it yourself, even when meeting your needs involves building and using a compost toilet.

But, there are advantages to a DIY composting toilet. They might smell terrible, but they are very cheap to make and they don't require any water for flushing, so you don't have to worry about providing water for your toilet from your finite water supply.

The silver lining is that they are very easy to make. You only really need a toilet seat, a bucket, and some wood shavings. However, they can be very smelly and you don't want to end up in a situation where the bucket tips. So you can design an outdoor toilet that looks similar to a cupboard with doors.

The doors keep the smell away and leave everything contained. Also, make sure that you change the bucket regularly (every 2-3 days) and add wood shavings to the feces after every use.

We recommend that you add a urine diverter to your DIY composting toilet. Feces compost much quicker when dry, so you want to keep urine away from it. A urine diverter sounds very fancy, but it is just a funnel added to the front of the toilet bowl, on the inside, to catch your urine in a urine chamber and keep it separate from feces. The urine chamber should be emptied every 2-3 days. You have the option to then treat your urine separately or to use it as a source of nitrogen for your garden.

As a word of caution, you need very high temperatures to kill all the pathogens in blackwater compost. We advise that you purchase a composter, otherwise it can take up to two years without high temperatures to treat your compost.

2. Septic Tanks

Septic tanks can be placed underground and connected to your house through perforated pipes. They allow for oils and fats in the waste to rise to the top and for solids to sink to the bottom. Then, the wastewater by-product moves on to the second section, where it flows out through your garden irrigation system into the "leach field", i.e. your garden's soil. The soil then does the job of breaking down and filtering the water while the fats and solids remain in the tank.

With most septic systems, you need to empty them out (pumping them out) every 3 to 5 years.

A survival party with 3-4 people will need a septic tank that can hold 1,000 gallons (between 90-120 inches long and 60-80 inches wide). You will also need to lay the pipes in your leach field, so your leach field needs to measure about 4,500 square feet (about 100 feet long and 45 feet wide).

Do not install your septic system yourself. While it is possible to do so, using a professional gives you the reassurance that they have done it properly. The last thing you want during a disaster is to have your septic tank burst, with no professional to help you deal with it. Not to mention, you just simply cannot take your chances with things like human waste. If they contaminate your food and water supply, it could kill you within the space of just a few days. In this case, you do not want to take any chances!

You will also be most likely required by law to have it inspected before use. As you can imagine, failing inspections over and over again is expensive. Some states and municipalities require that your septic tank be installed by a professional. It simply is in your best interest to hire a professional from the outset.

3. Aerobic System

Aerobic systems are similar to septic tanks, except it is divided into 6 or 7 sections. The first 2-3 sections use the same anaerobic breakdown process as a septic tank. In the last sections, oxygen is pumped in to help the bacteria in the waste break it down through an aerobic process. Unlike a septic tank, you get much cleaner water that is then released into the soil.

Thanks to its added sections, septic tanks need more parts and upkeep and are more expensive. However, they are definitely worth it if you can afford one.

Before choosing what off-grid wastewater and waste management system you want to implement, check your local laws! There may be restrictions and requirements that you must abide by. If you feel that the restrictions and requirements are unlawful, then you can mount a legal challenge.

How To Get An Off-Grid Water Supply Without A Well

In case you don't have access to a well, collecting rainwater is the next best alternative.

Most people don't know that just one inch of rain falling on an area measuring about 1,000 square feet can yield up to 600 gallons. The Environmental Protection Agency (EPA, 2022) states that the average American home uses 300 gallons of water daily. Unfortunately, it does not rain every day.

If you were to collect all the water that fell on your roof in all of 2019, you could only collect 59,126 gallons of rainwater (Off-Grid Home, 2022a). That means you can only get half of your annual water needs from rainwater. In that case, conserving and managing your collected rainwater is paramount to survival. You will also need to:

- Reduce the amount you use. You can take a shower every two days instead of daily, for example.

- Recycle water using the greywater tips discussed in this chapter.

- Create a larger area for rain collection by using frames and tarps.

- Supplement rainwater by buying some water or finding an alternative source, like a river.

The good news is that a rainwater system has many variables. That means that you can set it up to suit your property, as well as the resources you have available. Four ways to collect rainwater are:

1. **The Roof**

Clean the gutters around the lower edges of your roof area or install gutters if you have none.

Install filters in the gutters and in the downpipe.

Add a first flush diverter to your downpipe to divert the first few gallons of dirty water that run off your roof.

Place a container below your downpipe to catch the water.

2. **Tarp**

Dig a basin-shaped hole in the ground, about a few inches deep to match the size and shape of your tarp.

Make sure the hole is lower in one corner to create a flow.

Lay your tarp into the hole, ensuring the edges curve up to prevent water from running off the edge.

Run a pipe or rigid hose from the lower corner into a container.

3. Frame

Create a large, inclined, smooth surface, such as rigid plastic sheeting, and hold it off the ground using a rigid frame. Add guttering at the lower edge to collect the rainwater into your collection container.

4. Direct Container

Place as many open containers outside as possible to collect rainwater. Empty them regularly, to prevent algae from growing and to keep mosquitoes away.

5. Rainwater Above-Ground

Store your rainwater in big above-ground storage containers. If possible, place it next to your house or on a rooftop/elevated surface. That way, minimal piping, and guttering are needed.

SURVIVAL TASK

Think about which system you think is most appropriate for you to get. How quickly could you get it fitted? How would each different element fit into your emergency plan? For example, if the plan was to move to another safe location, then would it be more effective to install an off-grid waste management system where your safe location is?

Never use light-colored containers, as the sunlight on the container will cause algae to grow. Use opaque black or green containers instead. In cold weather, wrap the heating tape around your containers and pipes to prevent your water from freezing.

Collecting rainwater is cheap because, apart from the price of containers - which are affordable - you can swap full containers for empty ones to collect more water (if you keep your storage above ground).

Key Chapter Takeaway

- Greywater is separated from blackwater because it contains less waste, such as dirt, food waste, human skin cells, and cleaning products.

- Greywater only needs minimal treatment before you can reuse it in your garden and even toilet bowls.

- Blackwater waste has much more pathogens and bacteria in it because it contains more harmful waste, including urine and feces.

- Before choosing what off-grid wastewater and waste management system you want to implement, check your local laws! There may be restrictions as well as requirements that you must abide by.

- In case you don't have access to a well, collecting rainwater is the next best off-grid alternative.

In the next chapter, you will learn the importance of being prepared for any scenario, particularly when it comes to protecting yourself and your loved ones.

Chapter Nine: Protecting Yourselves

This chapter aims to highlight the importance of being prepared for any scenario, particularly for protecting yourself and your loved ones. You will learn how to know your enemy, use lethal and non-lethal tools, as well as DIY weapons, and use defensive tactics under fire.

Six Things Not to Do

Here are six things a good prepper never does in order to stay safe:

1. **Bragging About Your Supply**

The first thing any seasoned prepper will tell you is to never share with others that you are a prepper. In times of desperation, anyone can turn against you. Protect yourself by keeping your prepper status secret and sharing only with people who are in your survival party.

2. Relying on One Form of Defense

Remember that a good prepper always has a Plan A, Plan B, and Plan C. So practice and prepare to use more than one form of defense, from hand-to-hand combat to guns, to non-lethal weapons.

3. Only Stockpiling Guns and Ammo

Lethal weapons are not needed in every scenario. Sometimes you can deescalate a situation with non-lethal weapons, so it is best to stockpile other forms of weapons apart from guns and ammo.

4. Not Bugging Out

No matter how much you try to defend or protect your house, you may need to leave if it is compromised by enemies. Always have a packed bug-out bag ready to leave at a moment's notice.

5. Shooting on Sight

Not everyone approaching you or your shelter is an enemy. Someone may just be approaching for help or out of curiosity. Resist the urge to shoot on sight, as it can just escalate a situation badly. Always have the mentality that you are protecting yourself, not attacking others.

6. Not Defending Your Home Well Enough

As we've seen in chapter 6, there are severe consequences for not defending your home well enough, so don't make this mistake.

Knowing Your Enemy

Knowing your enemy and defending yourself from your enemy is pivotal for survival. But who is your enemy? That's the worrying part about shit hitting the fan: anyone can be your enemy, be it looters, hungry beggars, or thirsty neighbors who find out you have water. Other potential enemies include rioters and organized gangs. The great news is that, if you take the precautions listed in **chapter 6**, as well as those listed in this chapter, you can protect yourself if the time comes.

Non-Lethal Tools

Here are some non-lethal tools you can keep on hand for self-defense.

1. **Bear Spray**

Bear spray is just pepper spray for bears. If sprayed near a bear, the bear will most likely stay away from you and even leave because they could not breathe.

2. **Stun Gun and Taser**

Check your state and local laws to ensure that owning a stun gun and taser is legal. If it is then purchase both. Stun guns require direct contact (i.e. being physically close to the assailant), while tasers work even a few feet from your assailant.

3. **Pepper Spray**

Pepper spray is one of the best non-lethal weapons out there. Once you use it on an assailant, they cannot breathe and it burns their eyes severely. This gives you enough time to escape. You also don't need to be close to a person to use pepper spray. You can be a few feet away from them.

4. Kubotan

Learn how to use the Kubotan in self-defense. While it requires you to be close to the assailant, you can purchase one with a pepper spray that enables you to stay far from your assailant. It allows you to incapacitate them with the pepper spray before you then approach them and use your Kubotan on them.

Lethal Tools

If a person appears as though they intend to harm you, then you are well within your right to use a lethal tool against them.

1. Firearms in Restrictive States

If you live in a restrictive state, you can still carry a pump shotgun or a lever-action rifle in a mid-weight cartridge.

2. **Firearms in Open States**

In open states, carry semi-automatic pistols and rifles. They are the most reliable guns against someone who wants to harm you.

3. **DIY Weapons**

In case you don't have the above weapons on you, you can make your own DIY weapons, like:

- Spears
- Blowguns
- Primitive Club Tools
- Balloon Slingshots
- Stun Grenades

Defensive Tactics When Under Fire

Here are some defensive tactics you can use when under fire:

- Force Dispersal
- Fanning Out

- Positioning along a diagonal line
- Protective tactics for your family
- Weaponry
- Codes/safety systems

Survival Task

Now that you have everything to defend yourself, you can complete the next task. This is a very important task as part of the preparation required for catastrophe, so don't skip it.

First, recap this chapter. Reflect on why defense is important, but also think about what defense is right for you. If you are not comfortable shooting people, then it may be better to concentrate on non-lethal weapons, for example.

Next, do a stock check. What weapons do you already have? What weapons do you still need? Things like kitchen knives can come in very handy, so don't forget them. Using the template below, create a list of the weapons you currently have and take stock of what you need to do to get really prepared.

Firearms	**Other Lethal Weapons**	**Non-Lethal Weapons**

Key Chapter Takeaway

- Knowing your enemy and defending yourself from your enemy is pivotal for survival.

- Worryingly, when shit hits the fan, anyone can be your enemy.
- If a person seems as though they want to harm you, then you are well within your right to use a lethal tool against them.
- Not everyone who approaches you is an enemy. Try not to use lethal weapons unless you are sure they want to harm you.

In the next chapter, you will learn how to create an emergency plan, whether this is just for yourself or for your entire survival party.

CHAPTER TEN: CREATING AN EMERGENCY PLAN

Now that you have all the tools you need to create an emergency plan—whether for you, your family, or anyone else in your survival party—you must spend time carefully creating your emergency plan to meet the needs of everyone in your party. This plan could, ultimately, be the difference between life and death in a life-threatening catastrophe.

As you create your plan, always keep in mind that you need to ***P.O.P***!

- ***P***lan, plan, plan!
- ***O***rganize your plans!
- ***P****ractice* drills!

Don't worry if you don't know how to create or organize your emergency plan. That is why we are here.

THE GOALS FOR YOUR EMERGENCY PLAN

There are four major goals that your emergency plan aims to achieve:

1. **Staying Safe**

A prepper is firstly concerned with survival. Well, how do you survive? By staying safe. Your plan must consider safety at every step. How do you drink safe, clean water when you're bugging out? Do you fortify your house against intruders? What do you pack in your first aid kit to meet the health needs of everyone in your survival party? Remember that your emergency plan must be tailored to meet the needs of everyone in your survival party.

2. **Limiting Loss**

There is no point storing a year's supply of food only to find that it has been damaged or infested with pests.

Prepping costs money, so you want to limit your losses. Otherwise, you are throwing money away.

3. Reuniting Quickly

Your emergency plan will have details of where to meet in case your survival party is separated.

4. Resuming Normal Life ASAP

The life of a prepper is difficult and requires a lot of resilience. You will want to prepare how to transition back into normal life ASAP.

8 Steps For Creating An Emergency Plan

Here are eight easy steps for creating an emergency plan:

1. Plan Now

As has been discussed in this book, disaster can strike at any moment. Trust us! You will regret not planning now if disaster strikes tomorrow.

2. **Assess What Will Happen**

What could realistically happen based on where you live? You don't expect a person who lives in Australia to prep for a snowstorm. So, what are the likely scenarios to occur in your area, whether political or societal upheaval or natural or manmade disasters?

3. **Communicate With Family and Friends**

There is no point in making a survival plan for your friends and family and not informing them of it. If the goal is for them to survive, then they must study your plan as well as have input in its creation.

4. **Make a Shelter and Secure Your Home**

As has been discussed in previous chapters, you will need to include in your plan details for making a shelter and securing your home. If there are any shelters you can make now or any way you can secure your home now, then you will also need to do that.

5. **Know How Long Supplies Will Last**

Your plan should account for how long supplies will last. Food is precious in an emergency and you can't just eat as you would. Rationing and planning will go a long way in keeping you alive.

6. **Have Books/Resources on Survival Skills**

As we said in the introduction, the prepping community is still relatively new. There is so much to learn, with information constantly being released. It is in your best interest to keep up with the community by reading books, visiting websites, and watching videos made by other preppers.

7. **Keep Your Plan Flexible**

You should have several unique plans for different scenarios. Ideally, you will have at least one plan for bugging out and one plan for bugging in. Your plan should be flexible enough that you can still follow it should detail change. If you plan to survive on your bean rations for three months and it runs out after the second month, you should be able to find another protein source in your food stockpile to last you the next month.

8. Keep Your Information Safe

In today's world, when you need your identification documents to do practically everything, you want to ensure that you keep your identity documents safe. The best way to do this is to scan them onto an online drive. This way, you always have electronic copies, in case you lose physical copies.

Second, always leave them stored securely in your bug-out bag in waterproof bags. That way, if you ever need to leave home, you will have your identity documents with you. You may need them to cross a border, for example.

Everyone in your survival party must also keep a small booklet with the contact information of everyone else. In case of separation, this booklet might be the one thing to reunite you. This contact information should also be stored in the online drive, along with identity documents.

In addition, everyone's bug-out bag must have physical copies of the emergency plan. It gives everyone time to study and familiarize themselves with it. The plan must also contain details of emergency meeting places for everyone in your survival party. You must decide on a primary and secondary meeting place, in case of separation. In your plan, there must also be details of your out-of-area meeting place.

ORGANIZING YOUR PLAN

Most preppers like to use binders to organize their plan. You can then place these binders in important locations, such as your car, office, your children's locker at school, and your bug-out bags.

If you have kids, encourage them to read the plan and become familiar with worst-case scenarios so that, if an emergency strikes, they won't panic. Instead, they could go straight into action.

Your binder should contain:

- Contact information of everyone in your survival party. In addition, include the contact information of other people that you know, for example, grandparents, neighbors, teachers, and anyone and everyone who may be of help during a disaster

- Include all allergy and medical information in binders
- Response plans to likely scenarios in your area
- Responsibilities of everyone in your survival party. If disaster strikes, who puts out the containers to collect rainwater? Who unplugs all devices in the house? Create a list of necessary tasks
- Make physical copies of personal identification documents such as passports and driver's licenses
- Food storage information, including expiry date and how much food you have
- Details (and maps) of emergency meeting places

Last, practice drills with everyone in your survival party. This is a great way to prevent anyone from freezing out of shock and, ultimately, not surviving as a result

SURVIVAL TASK

This book has given you the knowledge you need to now write an in-depth plan for any catastrophe. Your best tool for survival is this plan. Once you've thought every detail through, you will be completely prepared to adapt to multiple situations that could happen. When things go wrong, this will be your most valuable asset.

Key Chapter Takeaway

- Your emergency plan could, ultimately, be the difference between life and death in a life-threatening catastrophe.
- Organize your plan in binders, then place them in strategic locations, such

as your car, office, or children's school lockers.

In the next chapter, you will do a final check-in. Now that you have read the book, you know exactly what to do when things go wrong.

CHAPTER ELEVEN: A FINAL CHECK-IN

This chapter is your final preparation phase. Once you have completed this check-in exercise, you will know exactly what you need to do to become more prepared and live off the grid, should the need for it arise.

CHECK-IN EXERCISE

Now you have finished the book, let's first explore where you are right now in your prepping for the worst-case scenario journey.

Below, rate yourself on a scale of 1 - 5 on how accurate the statements are for you. A score of 1 means "not accurate," and a score of 5 means "very accurate." After you have rated yourself according to the statements, add the total of your scores, then read "What Your Score Really Means" to determine the outcome of your results.

Check-in Statement

Check-in Statement	Self-Rating
I am completely sure that I can live off-grid.	
I have a detailed idea of what it takes to be self-sufficient.	
My bug-out bag contains everything I need to survive for 3 days.	
I know where I will source water and how to purify it.	
I have stored food for emergencies and am now food self-sufficient.	
I have decided whether it is best for me to bug-in bug-out. I know	

how to fortify my home for bugging in and how to create my own bunker or shelter for bugging out.	
I have a basic knowledge of first aid to treat either myself or my family.	
I know how to create a basic off-grid waste system.	
I know how to keep myself safe from enemies during disasters.	
I have an emergency plan for any disaster scenario that could happen right now.	
TOTAL SCORE:	

What Your Score Really Means

Score: 10-15

You are not prepared for a disaster and will struggle to keep yourself and your family safe during an emergency.

Did you skip any chapters? Maybe you should have another read...

Score: 16 - 30

You have a basic understanding of what it means to be a prepper, but you should review your strategies and make changes to enhance your preparedness.

Well done! This is definitely good progress. Draw up a plan of how you can even better your knowledge. Review any chapters you were a little unsure about and make sure your plan is perfect.

Score: 31+

You are almost ready for survival during a disaster! Review your plans to ensure they are ready to go.

Great job. You have put yourself in a powerful position for any catastrophe that may occur.

Don't be discouraged if you haven't scored well. Reread the sections you scored low on to fully understand the information and get back on track to being prepared.

If you scored well in this check-in exercise, then congratulations are in order! You are now fully prepared for survival in the case of a disaster!

FINAL WORDS

This has been a long journey, but you finally made it: you have all the information that you need to survive when shit hits the fan. From experience, we know how empowered you must feel knowing that you can survive no matter what happens. This is not a feeling that most people get to experience. You certainly deserve to enjoy your accomplishment because it took a lot of work and guts to get through this book. Congratulations!

As you go on to implement all the survival guides that we have brought you, we hope you keep in mind that you are doing this for your survival and the survival of your loved ones. All the hard work will pay off!

You may find that, as you begin to store your food and prepare for water shortages, family and friends will become more interested and invested in prepping too. You are simply a trendsetter who will go on to save the lives of many.

The great news is that you now have all this knowledge to share with others around you who may become interested in prepping, from how to pack a bug-out bag, to how much water to store for survival; how to source water, purify water, and how to store food properly to survive for months and even years!

You even know how to cook without power and how to build your oven as a long-term cooking solution. As if that's not enough, you now know how to build temporary shelters and your underground bunker. You know how to pack a survival first aid kit and how to secure your home against intruders.

Last, you know how to create off-grid waste systems and how to protect yourself from anyone or any animal that may want to attack you. You have a detailed emergency plan and you know the importance of sticking to it. Even better, you have the tools that you need in case you need to deviate from your emergency plan.

You are now prepared to face the unknown and deal with what could be a major catastrophe, so remember to keep this guide handy for hints and tips when SHTF.

We leave you one last piece of advice: disaster can strike at any moment, so always stay prepared. In the words of the great Carl Sagan, "Extinction is the rule. Survival is the exception."

DID YOU ENJOY THE BOOK? WE'D LOVE TO HEAR YOUR THOUGHTS!

Thank you for purchasing & reading our book! We do have a favor to ask from you, and that's if you can leave a review on our Amazon page!

As a small, independent publishing company with a tiny marketing budget, reviews are our livelihood on this platform. Even if it's just a sentence or two, it would make all the difference and would be very much appreciated.

If you already have, we'd like to thank you so much for leaving the review!

If you haven't yet, you can simply write your review here on our page through one of these links or scan the QR Codes.

If you're from the US, you can leave a review by clicking this link or scanning the code:

https://amazon.com/review/create-review?&asin=9781804210079

If you're from the UK, you can leave a review by clicking this link or scanning the code:

https://amazon.co.uk/review/create-review?&asin=9781804210079

We pour our heart and soul into our books, and reviews like yours help us spread our message and get our work into the hands of more people.

We appreciate you, and we just want to say thank you.

Sincerely,

Small Footprint Press

REFERENCES

Alexa, R. (2021, May 2). Bugging In: How To Fortify Your Home For SHTF. Tactical. https://www.tactical.com/fortify-your-home-shtf/.

Alexa, R. (2018, April 18). Should You Bug In Or Bug Out When SHTF? Tactical. https://www.tactical.com/should-you-bug-in-or-bug-out/.

Berkey Filters. (2022). Berkey Filter Test Results. Berkey Filters. https://www.berkeyfilters.com/pages/filtration-specifications.

BigRentz Inc. (2020, July 20). How To Build An Underground Bunker In 9 Steps. Big Rentz. https://www.bigrentz.com/blog/how-to-build-underground-bunker.

Blair, C. (2022). How Long Can Water Be Stored Before it Goes Bad? EZ Prepping. https://ezprepping.com/how-long-can-water-be-stored-before-it-goes-bad/.

Bryant, R. (2014). Defensive Tactics When Under Fire. The Prepper Journal. https://theprepperjournal.com/2014/08/29/defensive-tactics-fire/amp/.

Bug-Out Bag Builder. (2022). Bug-Out Bag Builder Checklist. https://www.bugoutbagbuilder.com/sites/default/files/images/Bug-Out-Bag-Builder-Checklist.pdf.

Burton-Hughes, L. (2017, May 17). What Are 'The Big 8' Food Allergies? High Speed Training. https://www.highspeedtraining.co.uk/hub/common-food-intolerances-allergies/.

Collier, E. (2019, August 26). What Are The Four Types Of Food Contamination? High Speed Training. https://www.highspeedtraining.co.uk/hub/four-types-contamination/.

Conroy, J.O. (2020, April 30). We Mocked Preppers And Survivalists - Until The Pandemic Hit. The Guardian. https://www.theguardian.com/global/2020/apr/30/preppers-survivalists-disasters-lessons.

Denzer, K. (2022). Build Your Own Wood-Fired Earth Oven. Mother Earth News. https://www.motherearthnews.com/diy/build-your-own-wood-fired-earth-oven-zmaz02onzgoe/.

Emergency First Response Corp. (2022). 5 Reasons Why Basic First Aid Knowledge Is Essential. Emergency First Response Corp. https://www.emergencyfirstresponse.com/5-reasons-why-basic-first-aid-knowledge-is-essential/.

Engel Fires. (2018, October 26). The Benefits Of Wood Fired Cooking. Engel Fires. https://www.engelfires.co.nz/blog/benefits-wood-fired-cooking.

Gamble, E. (2020, August 21). 5 Reasons Why You Need A Bug-Out Bag. Eric Gamble. https://www.ericgamble.com/5-reasons-why-you-need-a-bug-out-bag/.

Global Water Group. (2022). Difference Between Blackwater And Greywater. Global Water Group. https://www.globalwatergroup.com.au/our-blog/difference-between-blackwater-and-greywater.

Happy Preppers. (2022). Bleach Storage Tips For Beginners. Happy Preppers. https://www.happypreppers.com/bleach.html.

Happy Preppers. (2022). First Aid Kits. Happy Preppers. https://www.happypreppers.com/First-aid.html.

Happy Preppers. (2022). Prepper Medicine Cabinet. Happy Preppers.https://www.happypreppers.com/medicine-cabinet.html.

Happy Preppers. (2022). Water Survival Guide. Happy Preppers. https://www.happypreppers.com/water.html.

Jones, K. (2022). Be Part Of The Solution: 14 Compelling Reasons To Be A Prepper. The Provident Prepper. https://theprovidentprepper.org/be-part-of-the-solution-14-compelling-reasons-to-be-a-prepper/.

Kimble, B. (2022). 9 Celebrity Preppers Ready For Anything. Ready Wise. https://readywise.com/blogs/readywise-blog/9-celebrity-preppers-ready-for-anything.

Kylene. (2022). Be Part Of The Solution: 14 Compelling Reasons To Be A Prepper. The Provident Prepper. https://theprovidentprepper.org/be-part-of-the-solution-14-compelling-reasons-to-be-a-prepper/.

Kylene. (2022). Emergency Water: 17 Potential Sources. The Provident Prepper. https://theprovidentprepper.org/emergency-water-17-potential-sources/

Kylene. (2022). Ingenious Places to Store Your Emergency Food Supply. The Provident Prepper. https://theprovidentprepper.org/ingenious-places-to-store-your-emergency-food-supply/.

Kylene. (2022). Steps To Build A Successful Family Emergency Plan. The Provident Prepper. https://theprovidentprepper.org/steps-to-build-a-successful-family-emergency-plan/.

Kylene. (2022). Top 10 Foods To Hoard For "The End of The World As We Know It". The Provident Prepper. https://theprovidentprepper.org/top-10-foods-to-hoard-for-the-end-of-the-world-as-we-know-it/.

Lussier, M. (2018, May 30). 5 Reasons To Grow Your Own Food. University Of New Hampshire. https://www.unh.edu/healthyunh/blog/nutrition/2018/05/5-reasons-grow-your-own-food.

Mel C. (2021, June 4). The Get Home Bag Vs. The bug-out Bag Vs. The Go Bag. Tactical. https://www.tactical.com/get-home-bag-vs-bug-out-bag-vs-go-bag/.

Merriam-Webster. (2022). Bug-Out Bag. Merriam-Webster. https://www.merriam-webster.com/dictionary/bug-out%20bag#:~:text=Definition%20of%20bug%2Dout%20bag,rapid%20evacuation%20%3A%20go%20bag%20When%20%E2%80%A6.

Mr BOBB. (2016, April 11). How To Build A $20 Budget Friendly Bug Out Bag. Bug-Out Bag Builder.

https://www.bugoutbagbuilder.com/blog/best-20-budget-bug-out-bag-build.

Mr BOBB. (2019, August 26). Survival Self-Defense Weapons For Prepper's. Bug-Out Bag Builder. https://www.bugoutbagbuilder.com/blog/survival-self-defense-weapons-preppers.

Off-Grid Home. (2022). The Complete Guide To Off-Grid Wastewater Management. Off-Grid Home. https://off-grid-home.com/guide-to-off-grid-wastewater/.

Off-Grid Home. (2022). How To Get An Off-Grid Water Supply Without A Well. Off-Grid Home. https://off-grid-home.com/how-to-get-an-off-grid-water-supply/.

OHare, M. (2019, June 14). Spending Time In Nature Boosts Health, Study Finds. CNN. https://edition.cnn.com/travel/article/nature-health-benefits/index.html.

Preissman, D. (2017, June 28). How To Choose The Ultimate Bug Out Location. Tactical. https://www.tactical.com/how-to-choose-the-ultimate-bug-out-location/.

Preissman, D. (2017, June 28). What's A Bug Out Location? Tactical. https://www.tactical.com/how-to-choose-the-ultimate-bug-out-location/.

Preparedness Advice. (2020, November 26). Preppers Food Storage 101: An Ultimate Guide. Preparedness Advice. https://preparednessadvice.com/prepper-food-storage/.

Primed Preppers. (2022). Prepper Water Storage And Filtration - The Ultimate Guide. Primed Preppers. https://primedpreppers.com/prepper-water-storage-filtration/.

Rich, M. (2015, November 15). What You Really Need In Your SHTF First Aid Kit. Ask A Prepper. https://www.askaprepper.com/what-you-really-need-in-your-shtf-first-aid-kit/.

Schuaf, C. (2022, March 2). Bug-Out Bag Essentials Checklist. Uncharted Supply. https://unchartedsupplyco.com/blogs/news/bug-out-bag-checklist.

SHTFDad. (2022). 10 Reasons To Build An Underground Bunker. SHTFDad.

https://www.shtfdad.com/10-reasons-to-build-an-underground-bunker/.

Sullivan, D.F. (2022). 16 Surprising Benefits Of Prepping. Survival Sullivan. https://www.survivalsullivan.com/16-surprising-benefits-of-prepping/.

Sullivan, D.F. (2022). 7 Kick Ass DIY Weapons For Your Survival. Survival Sullivan. https://www.survivalsullivan.com/7-kick-ass-diy-weapons-for-your-survival/.

Sullivan, D.F. (2022). Bug-Out Shelters. Survival Sullivan. https://www.survivalsullivan.com/bug-out-shelters/.

Sullivan, D.F. (2022). Why Shelter Is Important. Survival Sullivan. https://www.survivalsullivan.com/why-shelter-is-important/.

Survivalist 101. (2022). Emergency Water Storage: How Much Water To Store For Prepping? Survivalist 101. https://survivalist101.com/tutorials/preppers-guide-prepping-for-beginners/emergency-water-storage-how-much-water-to-store-for-prepping/.

Survivalist 101. (2022). How To Cook Food Without Power. Survivalist 101. https://survivalist101.com/tutorials/preppers-guide-prepping-for-beginners/how-to-cook-food-without-power/.

The Bug-Out Bag Guide. (2022). How To Make A Bug-Out Plan. The Bug-Out Bag Guide. https://www.thebugoutbagguide.com/how-to-make-a-bug-out-plan/.

The Prepared Way. (2019, August 19). Home Security For Preppers—Protecting Your Home And Family After SHTF. https://thepreparedway.com/home-security-for-preppers-protecting-your-home-and-family-after-shtf/.

The Prepper Journal. (2022). WROL—Protecting Your Family When The Bad Guys Come Down Your Street—Pt. 1. The Prepper Journal. https://theprepperjournal.com/2013/08/29/without-rule-of-law-protecting-your-family-when-the-bad-guys-come-pt-1/amp/.

The Prepping Guide. (2022). Prepping Basics: How To Start Prepping in 2021. The Prepping Guide. https://thepreppingguide.com/prepping-basics/.

The Provident Prepper. (2022). Emergency Cooking—Recommended Products. The Provident Prepper. https://theprovidentprepper.org/recommended-products/emergency-cooking-recommended-products/.

The Provident Prepper. (2022). SHTF Plan: How to Create Your Survival and Emergency Plans. The Provident Prepper. https://thepreppingguide.com/shtf-plan/.

The Smart Survivalist. (2022). Off Grid Septic System And Sanitation: The How-To Guide. The Smart Survivalist. https://www.thesmartsurvivalist.com/off-grid-septic-system-and-sanitation-the-how-to-guide/.

UK Preppers Guide. (2017, September 26). Safety First Aid For Preppers. UK Preppers Guide.

https://www.ukpreppersguide.co.uk/safety-first-aid-for-preppers/.

Urban, A. (2022). The Beginner's Guide To Emergency Food Storage. Urban Survival Site. https://urbansurvivalsite.com/beginners-guide-to-emergency-food-storage/.

Urban Survival Network. (2022). 10 Common Prepping Mistakes Every Survivalist Should Avoid. Urban Survival Network. https://www.urbansurvivalnetwork.com/10-common-prepping-mistakes-every-survivalist-should-avoid/.

Vukovic, D. (2022, March 21). 22 Ways To Cook Without Electricity When The Grid Fails. Primal Survivor. https://www.primalsurvivor.net/ways-cook-without-electricity/.

Weston, J. (2021, April 15). 20 Items To Kick Start Your Long Term Food Storage Plan. Backdoor Survival. https://www.backdoorsurvival.com/20-items-to-kick-start-your-food-storage-plan/.

www.ingramcontent.com/pod-product-compliance
Lightning Source LLC
La Vergne TN
LVHW010940100826
845153LV00002B/101

9781804210086